May God bless!

THE COST OF CHANGE

THE COST OF CHANGE

What to Expect
When You're in Transition

MARCUS D. KING

The Cost of Change: What to Expect When You're in Transition
by Marcus D. King

Cover Design by Atinad Designs.

SAINT PAUL PRESS, DALLAS, TEXAS

First Printing, 2015

ISBN-10: 1519110596
ISBN-13: 978-1519110596

Printed in the U.S.A.

Contents

Preface

Change is going to happen in your life whether you like it or not. Since change is inevitable, you have a decision to make. You can sit back and complain about all the changes that are taking place in your life, or you can take change by the horns and ride through each transitional phase with an understanding of what you may expect each step of the way. If you choose the first option, you may not be as serious about making your life the best it can be as you say you are. However, if you are serious, you just may be having some challenges because you have not been mentored through certain seasons of your life where there were changes that upset everything you considered normal or comfortable.

When you purchased this book, you invested in a personal transitional mentor that will coach you through some of life's most challenging transitions by giving you principles that can be applied in your relationships, business, leadership, church and religious organizations as well as your personal life. You're about to take a journey through several transitions with a group of people and see how they managed each phase. There will be some phases that they encountered that will be right where you are in the present moment of your life. There will be others you are about to encounter in the next phase of your life. Then, you will be able to smile and celebrate because you will identify with the fact that you have successfully at some point in time walked through certain phases and have the battle scars to prove it. Whatever the case may be, you cannot escape the fact that you will always experience changes, but now you have a tool to help you walk with boldness and confidence through those unnerving transitions.

I've had changes in every single phase and level of my life from personal to business. Whether changing careers, ending and beginning new relationships, hiring and firing employees, painful health challenges, and being in various income levels, I've been there. I was not only there; I'm going through changes as I write this book. You know the great part about it all? I have more peace because I now know what principles to apply in almost every situation I may face in the future. You have read this far and that is great. Be bold and dare to change your life and give yourself the peace you deserve by transitioning to the first chapter through the last into a greater outlook on change for your future. Are you willing to pay the price?

1

Expect Changes When You're in Transition

I have watched several movies that you may be familiar with. Canadian-born actress Tatiana Maslany is known for her role in such movies as *The Entitled* and *The Vow*. She's very strategic in the roles she has taken. At age twenty-eight, she described how she sees changes in her life and the changing experiences in her career. Here's what she said during an interview: "I'm at the transition place myself, still playing high school girls, but moving to a stage [where] I'm playing older roles and going to the places of stillness, wisdom, knowledge, and weight." She goes on to say, "It's exciting and scary."

What she's saying is, 'I've been playing younger girls in my roles even though I am twenty-eight years old, but as I'm changing and transitioning in age, I will have to switch to more mature roles if I am going to remain relevant and grow in wisdom, knowledge, and expertise of what I have been created to do in this world.'

Here's what we need to understand: Tatiana expects changes in transition; it's part of the business. You go in understanding you cannot play the little girl all your life. You cannot play the young role all your life. She expects changes in her career as an actress.

Like Tatiana, God wants us to move from playing immature roles in our lives and move on in order to take on more mature roles. It's time to grow up. The challenge that comes with that is it usually takes us to places where we have to be still, know that He is God, and that we aren't controlling anything. I know you're educated; I know you have your degrees; I know you've actually done this before, but we have come to that place where God is about to stretch and grow us to another level where He says, 'I'm getting rid of certain roles. Even though you may still be in the same position, your role is going to be different in the next season.' We have to be still and know that He is God. When we do, we will grow in wisdom, we will grow in knowledge, and we will understand that the changes caused by the transition will make us people of greater substance. God does not want us to be shallow all of our lives.

When we talk about substance, it means we have greater weight in life. It means that when storms blow, we won't be blown away with the storm. We need to have some fortitude and stand our ground. 'After you've done all you can, just stand.'

Realize that transition can be scary and exciting all at the same time, but it is necessary. It is necessary for you to transition. It is necessary for you to change. It is necessary for things not to remain the same in your life for this simple reason: how boring life would be if nothing ever changed. How would you grow if nothing ever changed? So, as we examine the changes the Israelites went through, you will discover that there are four things we need to know that will help us navigate through the changes we must expect when we're going through transition. These are some things that should not catch us off guard as we are going through changes. God wants us to already be ahead of the game, because when you have His Word, He can give you foresight and insight on what's about to come in your sight.

Looking back to the chapters prior to Exodus 15, we see where God ended up calling a man by the name of Moses who was on the backside of the desert tending the sheep of Jethro, his father-in-law. God calls Moses for a time of change and transition in his life. Moses has now been called from leading sheep to leading people. God tells him to go tell Pharaoh, "Let My people go." In other words, God tells Moses to come out of his comfort zone and get away from what he had been doing all of these years. He [God] says, 'I know what you have become comfortable doing: You have become comfortable in this season of your life; you have been kicking back thinking that you are in retirement. You have forgotten that, as a child of God, retirement does not exist when God begins to call your name.' At eighty years of age, God says to Moses, 'It's time for you to take it to another level.' Right when you are ready to quit, God looks at you and says, 'Come here. I've let you rest for a couple of years, but right now, it isn't over; it's time to get the party started at another level.'

So, Moses is to go down and tell Pharaoh, "Let My people go." This is one of the most challenging things he has ever done in his life. However, before he gets there, Moses says to God, 'If I end up telling Pharaoh that, who will I tell him sent me?' God said, 'Let Me give you the password: Tell him 'I AM THAT I AM.' 'If you need backup, just say the Lord sent me. If he does not know who I am by the time I get through with him, he's going to recognize who I am by how I use you in his life.'

Moses ends up leading the children of Israel out of Egypt. They were now in transition. They were leaving their slavery situation and were running toward the Red Sea. As they were running toward the Red Sea, the Egyptians came chasing after them. They then come to a place where they had nowhere to turn. They could not go forward; they could not go right; they could not go left; they could not go back. Obeying God has brought them to a place where they are stuck, and they begin to think it is all over. Right when they thought it was all over, God opened up His "heavenly hydraulic system", pushed back the waters, and let them cross over on dry land. Often, in our lives, when we think it is over, God says, 'Watch Me do something you have never seen before.'

I don't know if this is referring to you, but you might feel trapped. However, God is telling you, 'I have you right where I need you to be because you have gone this far obeying Me, but this next level of your life is going to take Me doing something nobody has seen before.' You have never been this broke; you have never been this depressed; you have never been in this kind of situation in your life. With all your skills and degrees, you can't figure it out. Now you have to wait so God can work it out! Sometimes you have to move from what you know, and recognize who you know, and watch Him show up and do things you never thought He could do. There comes a point when we have reached the end of who we think we are so God can show us who He is. He opened up that Red Sea and the Israelites ran to the other side. Then, God closed up those same waters over the enemy causing them to drown so they could not affect His children any longer.

In Exodus 15:1-21, we see that the Israelites ended up writing a song about what they experienced. They begin to celebrate God and His goodness. They begin to tell about all He had done so much so that they all begin to sing the song. You have to understand that there are about a million people out there and they are all worshiping and praising God for what He had done. Isn't it something when all of God's people get on one accord, and everybody recognizes that, if it were not for the Lord, they would not be where they are? They could look back at that sea and recognize where they could have been—drowning or dead. Now they had a reason to give God praise, so they did what many people do—they put it in a song.

We see now that, as they come to this point, they begin

to understand that God is telling them, 'Alright, you have crossed the Red Sea to the other side. You're about to start a new era in your life. The reason I brought you out is because I'm taking you somewhere. I want you to go to the Promised Land, but here are some things you need to know on your journey to your destination. I need you to expect changes and here are four things you need to start expecting in this next season of your life.'

1. You Must Know What You Must Leave

The first thing you need to know is what you must leave. Where do I see this referenced? Look at verse 22: *"Then Moses led the people of Israel away from the Red Sea."* Notice with me what the children of Israel had to leave behind:

a) The place of their Crossing. God says, 'Alright, I allowed you to cross over.' Moses leads them away from the place they crossed over. The Israelites might be like the little boy whose parents tucked him in bed one night. After they prayed with him, the parents went to sleep. In the middle of the night, they heard a loud bump. They nervously stood up and ran around checking everything. They checked all the windows. They checked the doors. They checked everything, but they did not find anything that may have caused the bump. They then went into their son's room and found him laying on the floor. They looked at him and said, "Little Johnny, why in the world are you on the floor?" He said, "Maybe I stayed too close to where I laid into the bed."

God is saying to the Israelites, 'I brought you out of Egypt and across the Red Sea, but you're still too close. I don't want you tempted to cross back over when times get hard; you might fall because you're too close to what you just came out of. I don't want you so close to something you have been delivered from because you might be tempted to take a U-turn.'

You must know what you must leave. The Israelites had to leave their place of crossing.

b) The place of their Celebration. Look again at verse 22: *"Then Moses led the people of Israel away from the Red Sea."* Remember what they were doing at the Red Sea: they wrote a song about what God had just finished doing for them at the Red Sea. They were celebrating. And God says, 'I'm joining the celebration. I have to move you away from this place of celebration because you have work to do. You cannot party your entire time after you have crossed over from a challenging situation. Celebrate it, Israel! Celebrate it! Celebrate Me! Remember, don't get stuck at the Red Sea. Don't get stuck celebrating too long that you forget this was not your destination. This is just a layover on the way to where you are going. You can get so excited shouting at the Red Sea that you miss the Promised Land.' The Israelites had to leave their place of celebration.

c) The place of their Comfort. Israel is saying to God, 'What do You mean? Leave our place of comfort?' For the Israelites, it's comfortable by the Red Sea because God had just finished blessing them. Whenever God blesses you, you want to stay as close to what God just did because you're scared He might not do it again. You can get comfortable at the place where God blessed you. God is saying to you and me, 'I blessed you to get to this point, but don't stay comfortable. Don't start relaxing just because you crossed the Red Sea.'

One day, when I was growing up and learning how to swim, the lifeguard said, 'You need to push away from the side of the pool if you're ever going to learn how to swim in deep waters.' He said that because I had my life jacket on. When you have a life jacket on, you are covered. No matter how deep the water gets, you will always float to the top.

God is saying, 'Israel, you have to push away from the borders of the Red Sea because you're too comfortable. I didn't call you to hang out at the Red Sea. I called you to go to the Promised Land.'

If we are going to expect things, if we are going to expect changes in transition, we first need to know what we must leave.

2. You Must Know Where You Must Go

Verse 22 says, *"Then Moses led the people of Israel away from the Red Sea and they moved out into the desert of Shur."* What's going to happen next?

Has God ever told you to move to a place and it seemed like a sure place, but you weren't sure what was going to happen by the time you arrived there? God told the Israelites, 'Know where you must go.' Where did they have to go?

a) They had to go through a Dirty Season. In verse 22, God told them to go out into the desert of Shur. The last time I checked there was a whole lot of dirt in the desert. Everywhere they walked there was dirt all around them. The desert is dirty and dusty. They are surrounded by dirt. Dirt in their shoes. Dirt in their hair. Dirt in their stuff. They cannot escape the dirty season.

After they left the Red Sea, they had to walk in the wilderness of Shur for three days. They had to walk in the dirt for three days. No baths. No water. They're just walking in a dirty season.

b) They had to go through a Difficult Season. The Israelites have been delivered from the Red Sea, but they were delivered to go through dirt. They were delivered to go through difficulty. In the desert, during the day time, it is extremely hot, but when the night comes, it gets cold, and when it gets cold, all the critters and wild beasts begin to come out. All of these people had to watch their backs through this difficult season. God says, 'I delivered you, but you cannot stay at the Red Sea. You have to walk through the desert, through the dirt and the difficulties.

c) They had to go through a Dry Season. You're not going to see things as you want to see it. You're going to leave a place that is fruitful and enter into a season where nothing is coming your way. Every step you take you may see nothing, but dirt all around you. Everything around you is dry. God says, 'Listen, Israel, you're going to go through a dirty season; you're going to go through a difficult season; and now you must go through a dry season. You have to leave one place for Me to take you to another place.' The Israelites had to understand what they had to leave, where they had to go, and what they had to experience.

3. You Must Know What You Must Experience

Look again at verse 22: *"Then Moses led the people of Israel away from the Red Sea and they moved out into the desert of Shur; they traveled in this desert for three days without finding any water. When they came to the oasis of Marah, the water was too bitter to drink, so they called the place Marah which means bitter."* The Israelites faced another difficult experience during this transition time.

a) They need to experience not being able to Obtain something they really need. What do they need? They need water. They are not asking for more stuff, more horses, more chariots, or more food. Right now, all they need is water.

They traveled in the desert for three days without finding any water. Apparently, since our scriptures states they didn't find water, this must mean they were looking for water. It must mean that they had to be delivered from the Red Sea because God already knew this water (the Red Sea water) could not do them any good. All they can do is look at it because it's sea water, and if they drank this water, it would kill them on their way to their destiny. That is why God told them to leave where they were because it could not do them any good. I know it feels cool because there is a breeze by the water, but one day you are going to need to drink some water and what you need cannot be found in what you just crossed over. So, now they have been traveling for three days in this desert place; now they are looking for something they need.

They don't need any more stuff because when God allowed them to cross the Red Sea before they left Egypt, God moved the Egyptians to give them much gold and silver just to get them out of there. So, they have more gold, more bling, and more stuff than they have ever had in the last four hundred years. With all that stuff, they cannot find what they really need. They have what they want, but they don't have what they need. Have you ever been in a place where you have what you want, but you still don't have what you need? The Israelites were looking all over, but couldn't locate any water to drink. God was going to have to lead them to it.

b) They experience a Thirst they have never had before. Without water, they have a thirst that can't be quenched by anything else, and they are thirsty for this one thing that nobody else can give them. They are thirsty for this one thing that they have been doing without for a while. They could go back and drink sea water, but that is not the kind of water they need. That water will dehydrate them and kill them. They need something that will restore, refresh, and replenish them, and they have not run across it yet. Therefore, not being able to obtain something they need, they experience a thirst they have never had before.

c) They experienced an Emptiness they never had before. The Israelites could not find water and if we keep reading in Exodus 16, they apparently run out of something else. What good is it to have some food when you can't swallow it? What good is it to have bread to eat and you do not have anything to wash it down with? Now, they have an emptiness inside of them that they have never felt before, because even when they were in bondage with the enemy, they ate every day. At least when they were in prison, they had three square meals. They were able to eat even though it was the enemy's food.

The Israelites are now running out of time. They are under pressure. They cannot find what they need. They are thirsty like they have never been thirsty before, and now they have an emptiness inside of them—a void that cannot be filled.

God has said to them, 'You have to leave. You need to know where you are going, and you need to know what you will be experiencing.' There is a fourth thing that must be carried out during a period of transition.

4. You Must Keep the Right Perspective

The Israelites were delivered from Egypt, had celebrated at the Red Sea, but now were suffering in the desert without any water. Now, God wants them to keep the right perspective. How can you keep the right perspective through all of that? We see three things that happened to Israel.

In verse 23 we read: *"When they came to the oasis of Marah the water was too bitter to drink so they called the place Marah."*

a) They had a Bitter Experience. The Israelites have

already gone through challenging times in their life, and now it seems like they have finally found what they have been looking for. Remember, they are in the desert. They are thirsty; they are hungry. They are dried out; they are going through dirt—everything is going on that does not seem favorable. Now, while being in the midst of the desert, they see what they think is a mirage. Actually it was not a mirage; it was their reality. They saw an oasis in the desert. They are excited. They are elated. Their hopes have come up. They said, 'Oh, God has not forgotten us. Thank God, it's been only three days. We survived three days.'

Can you see them as they are walking towards the oasis? Let's see what happened next: When they get to the oasis they hurriedly scoop the water up into their hands and drink the water, but then they spit it out. The water isn't any good. Sometimes the person we have the most bitterness towards is God. Right now, it seems that God is playing with their emotions. The Israelites are probably thinking, 'You are going to let us run up on an oasis in this desert after traveling through this desert thirsty for three days? You delivered us from all of this other stuff we had to go through, and You are telling me, right now, we can't drink this?' Now they had a bitter experience. They had a bad taste in their mouth.

b) Something else they had to fight against in order to keep the right perspective was becoming a Bitter People. It's one thing to have a bitter experience, but it's another to become a bitter person. Look at verse 24: *"Then the people complained and turned against Moses. What are we going to drink?"* It wasn't Moses who delivered them. It was God and it was God who used Moses. Sometimes when you have delivered people or have helped people through a process in their life, if they don't get what they want like they want it in the next season, they'll turn on you in a heartbeat. Harriet Tubman said, "I could have freed more slaves if they had known they were slaves." Sometimes, the people you are trying to help the most are the ones who will hurt you the most, because they do not understand that you have been fighting on their behalf, and now you are in a fight with them. You are in no way trying to be a "prima donna"; you are trying to go through it because you listened to God. There are times, even though you listened to God, they are not listening to you because all they want their need to be met.

The Israelites became bitter because of the bitter water. Water in the Bible is symbolic of the Holy Spirit. Jesus ended up telling the woman at the well, 'I'll give you a drink, and you will never have to drink again (John 4:14)." Water is also symbolic of our spirit. In the Old Testament, we read of when God, through Elijah, had to make water good when the people could not drink from the water because it was bitter. This bitter water was a symbol that the whole land was bad (2 Kings 2: 19-22).

The Israelites had a bitter experience. They allowed the water that was outside of them, get inside of them. They did not control how they felt about the experience. They did not allow the experience make them better; they allowed it make them bitter. They became bitter because they had been waiting on this moment, and it did not go as planned. They are now losing their perspective.

Apparently, the only person who is not bitter after drinking the bitter water is Moses. Moses understands that if God brought them this far, there must be some better water somewhere. Moses knew that God would not leave His people to die after bringing them through the Red Sea situation. He knew that the bitter moment was just temporary.

c) The Israelites labeled their entire season a Bitter Place. Marah was just a spring in that region, but the Israelites began thinking of their whole experience as "bitter." Occasionally, if we have a bad experience at a location in one place, we label all locations of that place as bad. If you go to Red Lobster frequently, you might find that one time the fish was not cooked right. Instead of saying, 'Aw, they just had a bad day," you may say, 'I can't stand Red Lobster! As a matter of fact, I am never going to eat there again.' All Red Lobsters have now become a bitter place to you. We must be careful about labeling an entire season based on a single experience.

Are you going through a transition in your life? God may be telling you right now, 'You need to expect changes.' He may be saying, 'You need to know that there are some places you are going to have to leave. There are some people you will have to leave. There are some mindsets you will have to leave. There are some habits you will have to leave.'

When you have been delivered it is not enough just to be delivered; you have to manage your deliverance on the way to your Promised Land. You can be delivered and go right back to where you came from or die where you're staying if you don't know there is some stuff you have to leave behind. You have to learn how to forgive and leave stuff behind. If you keep on holding on to grudges, the 'cancer' inside of you will kill you because you did not know how to leave it behind.

You may have worked with a certain company for a long time, but God has set it up where He forced you out because He has been putting a vision of your life in your mind that is bigger than where you are. To transition to where God wants you to be, you have to leave that job behind. You may have to leave a relationship behind. You may have to leave a certain lifestyle behind. In order to get to where God wants you to go, you must be prepared to leave some things behind.

God had delivered the Israelites from Pharaoh's bondage, but guess what? When you have been in bondage for so long, it's hard for you to think for yourself when God finally frees you. You may resemble a bird who has been caged for a long time. If you open the cage, the bird won't fly anywhere, because it has been in bondage so long that it has become comfortable in the cage. God may be saying to you, 'It's time for you to fly.'

Whenever you cross over from one season to another, it's called graduation. The word we use to describe a graduation ceremony is "commencement." A commencement is not an ending; it is a beginning. You may have a new beginning today. God may be saying, 'This is the first day of the next season of your life.' He is getting ready to do some new things in your life.

How do you know that you are on the right road in your new season? Because you have to go through a dirty season. How do you know you are closer to your Promised Land? Because you have more dirt on you than you have ever had on you. You've had more lies told on you than you have ever had told on you before. You have more people in your business than you have ever had before. You have more pain than you have ever had before. That is why you should thank God for the dirty season, because if people really knew what you were made of, they would stop throwing dirt on you! If they knew that you were of the seed of Abraham, that you were of the seed of God, that you were of the seed of Jesus, they would realize that throwing dirt on you to try to stop you would be in vain. When they throw dirt on the seed, they're not burying you, they're preparing you to come out stronger. Be like Maya Angelou and say:

> You may write me down in history
> With your bitter, twisted lies,
> You may tread me in the very dirt
> But still, like dust, I'll rise.
>
> -'Still I Rise' (1978)

You have to go through a difficult season. I know this is not shouting material for some of you because you want things to always be the same. You don't want any battles. You don't want any fight. Here's the deal: if you can't be tested, you can't be trusted. If you think you are ready for what you think you are ready for, then you have to be tested.

God has to see how you respond to adversity at this level. New levels; new devils. They are going to come at you in ways you have never seen before, but if you have been tested, you can be trusted.

Can God trust you with trouble? He trusted Job with trouble. God had a conversation with the devil, and He told the devil, 'Job's not serving me for stuff. You can touch anything, but do not touch his body. Take his stuff. Take his family. Take his house, but at the end of the day, he's still going to trust Me.' Are you like Job who said, *"Though he slay me, yet will I trust in him (Job 13:15)"*? Are you like David who said, 'I will walk through the valley of the shadow of death because I know God is with me (Psalm 23:4)'?

You have to know what you are going to experience. You're going to search for what you really want, and you won't be able to find it. The reason you won't be able to find it is because in this season God wants you to find Him; and when you find Him, you will find what you want. Matthew 6:33 says, *"Seek ye first the kingdom of God and all His righteousness, and all other things shall be added unto you."*

When you get closer to God, your stuff will begin to come closer to you. Some things you need you cannot find and you become frustrated, but God does not let you have certain things because He's making you thirsty. He's making you hungry again. He's making you fast again. He's making you wake up in the middle of the morning and pray to Him like you have never prayed to Him before. He's saying, 'I want you to get up, get on your knees, and talk to Me. I'm calling you to another season. I'm calling you to a task you have never seen before. I'm calling you to greatness, but it takes you spending more time with Me. When you search for Me with all your heart, I will bless you in a way that you have never seen before.'

You have an emptiness in your life and God is going to fill it, but you have to know how to keep the right perspective. If you are not careful, when you have a bitter experience, and it leaves a bad taste in your mouth, you have to make sure you don't let what happened continue to happen to you. You can't keep rehearsing it, because the more you rehearse it, the more you keep speaking about it, and when you keep speaking about it, you speak it into your life. It begins to create a stronghold in your mind. The Bible says in Proverb 18:21, *"Death and life are in the power of the tongue."* Every time you talk about that bitter experience, you give it life. If you stop talking about it and start talking to God about your future instead of what happened to you in your past, God will help you get over your past and prepare for your future.

You cannot change what happened in the past. Let it go and start talking about your future. Don't become a bitter person. Bitterness and unforgiveness is like you drinking poison and waiting for the other person to die. It will corrupt your spirit. It will make every place you go bitter. You'll call the whole season that you are in bitter.

Here is how you keep the right perspective:

a) You have to know this is not the worst season of your life It's the best season of your life.
b) Even though you had a bitter experience, you're free in the bitter experience.

c) You're having a bitter experience on the other side of the Red Sea. If it doesn't work out, if you die now at least you won't die a slave. At least you'll die with your own mind. At least you'll die making your own decisions.
d) Even if you didn't get it right, you had the opportunity to do for yourself rather than having somebody dictate to you everything about your life.

The right perspective is God giving you an opportunity. You're on the side of the most pain you have ever had in your life, but do you know Jesus was there too? In Matthew 26:36-46 and Mark 14:32-42, Jesus was in the Garden of Gethsemane. He said, 'Father, if You can remove this bitter cup, then do it.' He had to put it in perspective. He said, 'I came for this. Not My will. Your will be done.' When you remember why God created you, you can go through anything. You can face the most painful 'cross' because you know that in three days you're going to have the greatest 'resurrection' ever! He never brought you this far to let you stay down because the ground is no place for a champion, and the grave is not a place for a living person. You have too much life in you to die right now.

> "Then Moses led the people of Israel away from the Red Sea, and they moved out into the desert of Shur. They traveled in this desert for three days without finding any water. When they came to the oasis of Marah, the water was too bitter to drink. So they

called the place Marah (which means "bitter").

Then the people complained and turned against Moses. "What are we going to drink?" they demanded. So Moses cried out to the Lord for help, and the Lord showed him a piece of wood. Moses threw it into the water, and this made the water good to drink.

It was there at Marah that the Lord set before them the following decree as a standard to test their faithfulness to him. He said, "If you will listen carefully to the voice of the Lord your God and do what is right in his sight, obeying his commands and keeping all his decrees, then I will not make you suffer any of the diseases I sent on the Egyptians; for I am the Lord who heals you."

After leaving Marah, the Israelites traveled on to the oasis of Elim, where they found twelve springs and seventy palm trees. They camped there beside the water."

Exodus 15:22-27 (NLT)

2

Expect Challenges When You're in Transition

All around us, people are in transition. Each year many are graduating from high school to college. Many are graduating from death to life. Many are graduating from singleness to marriage. Whatever the case, we're in transition. God is moving things around. One of two things is always going on: either people are being born into something, or people are transitioning out of something. Whoever you are, you're going through one of those things in your life right now. God is birthing you into something; or God is transitioning you out of something. I do not know where you are or who you are, but if you stay with God, you will be good either way.

As we begin to walk down this road of transition, we must understand what God is doing in our lives. Several things take place as we experience transition, and God does not want us caught off guard by these things. There are some things we need to expect during our transitional periods. One thing we ought to expect is change. Change can be both exciting and scary. Change can mess up your mind. But change can also stir excitement in you because you anticipate doing something new.

We have already discovered that, like the Israelites, there are four things we need to know that will help us navigate through the changes we must expect in transition. These things are:

1) **Know what we must Leave.** There are certain things that God is telling you to leave: there are some places you cannot stay; there are some relationships you cannot keep; there are some habits and attitudes you cannot hold on to.
2) **Know where we must Go.** Recognize that if God ever tells you to leave one place, He has already prepared another place. Don't be the one delaying your own destiny.
3) **Know what you must Experience.** We noticed that a bitter experience took place with the Israelites. Bitter experiences take place when we undergo changes. It is not always sweet when you end up in changing situations. If you say you are going to follow Christ, guess what? Following Christ is not all water-into-wine; it is also blood

on a cross. If you are going to follow Him, you have to follow Him all the way. The Bible says in 2 Timothy 2:12 *"If we don't suffer, we shall reign with Him."* We must follow Christ not just in the good times but also in the challenging times.

4) **Know how to keep the right Perspective.** When you go through challenging times, and you go through changes, you will not always see the light at the end of the tunnel. You will often feel that God has deserted you, or that you made the wrong choice. You will often feel as though everybody is against you, when the truth of the matter is, you have more people for you than against you. Sometimes all people may be against you, but when you have God on your side, you have a majority. The Bible says in Romans 8:31, *"If God is for us who can be against us?"* He's more than the whole world against us. If you have God on your side, and you keep the right perspective, you'll realize that God will never bring you out of something or lead you into something just to let you fail.

As we continue our journey with the Israelites, we'll discover that not only did they experience change, but they also had to face some major challenges along the way. These challenges were tailor-made for the Israelites, because whenever we are on a journey there are some challenges and changes that God will bring us through that are unique to us. That is why when you try to talk to other people about what you are going through, you will find that they may have gone through something similar, but they have not gone through the exact same thing. Only God knows how you truly feel. Although other folks may not understand you, "there is a friend that sticketh closer than a brother." Jesus has gone through every single thing we have gone through. He really knows what it means to walk beside each other and encourage each other. All we can say to others who are going through changes is, 'Even though I don't know exactly how you feel, I know that God will walk you through as He walked me through.'

During transitions, there are some unique challenges that we must face that other people won't experience. It's not about other people experiencing it; it's about us understanding what God is trying to do with this challenge that we face on our journey. There were some challenges that were unique to the Israelites during this particular journey on their way to the Promised Land out of Egypt. But God had chosen a particular leader for a particular time in this particular season, and only this leader could lead this people to go through these challenges at this time. This burden was heavy upon Moses.

As we move forward, we want to discuss and discover what Moses did when faced with challenges. Moses did not volunteer for these challenges; it was something God chose him for. God put the burden on his shoulders, and God was not letting up. We're about to find out what position Moses' choices end up putting God's people in, because whatever decisions Moses made, it was going to put the people whom he loved and cared for in a certain position. That is a heavy burden: to be responsible for people God gave you. Basically, God said to him, 'I'm giving you a burden. I'm giving you a responsibility, and you better get it right.' Sometimes the margin for error is zero. You don't have any room to mess up. I don't know your situation, but there's pressure on your life. And right now, if you don't make the right decision, it might be all over for you.

Let's do some background work. God heard the cry of His people. Moses was on the backside of the desert hanging with his father-in-law, Jethro, taking care of sheep. God called him and said, "Go tell Pharaoh, 'Let My people go.'" God allowed Moses to go down to Egypt. Moses went down and he ended up leading the people of Israel out of Egypt. Before they came out of Egypt, ten plagues fell upon Pharaoh and the Egyptians and he had to let the people go. God opened up the Red Sea and the Israelites ran across on dry ground. God drowned Pharaoh's army in the Red Sea. The children of Israel thanked God for all that had transpired, and they began to celebrate all that God had done. They wrote an entire song about what God had just done in their lives.

Then God says to them, 'Alright. Thank you for your song, but I didn't just call you and deliver you so you can sing a song by the Red Sea. I delivered you so you can head to the Promised Land.' God was letting them know, that just because they crossed over that did not mean they had made it. Just because you've been delivered, that does not mean you've reached your destiny. Don't stop short because you've had some victories. There is still work to do to accomplish the main goal that God has for your life.

As we look at our scriptures, we understand that Moses led the people away from the Red Sea and into the desert of Shur. They are now in the desert and have been in the desert for three days. They had to leave the Red Sea because they could not drink the water from the Red Sea. The people may have walked thirty miles within a three-day period. After journeying for three days, they became thirsty as they had run out of water. They ended up running into a spring (water), however it was not what they needed. They tasted the water, but the water was bitter. Thus, they called the whole place Marah. The whole place left a bitter taste in their mouths.

Without fresh water, the Israelites are in a challenging situation. Let's review our focus scripture again and see how they respond. Verses 23-24 state, *"When they came to the oasis of Marah, the water was too bitter to drink, so they called the place Marah which means bitter; then the people complained and turned against Moses."* Moses did not have to have Chris Brown; he just said these people aren't loyal. These same people who had followed Moses all the way from Egypt now have "spiritual amnesia." Because one thing did not go their way, they turned against Moses. They are asking, 'What are we going to drink?' You have to understand, Moses is in the same situation as they are. Moses is thirsty, also. They look at Moses and ask, 'What are we going to drink?' It's not like he was walking around with Gatorade in his pockets. He's sitting there with a million people asking him, 'What are we going to drink?' when he has that same issue. Oftentimes, followers do not understand that the leaders are going through the same thing they are going through. The followers' needs seem to be greater than everybody else's need, and the leader has to put aside his needs to make sure he takes care of the followers' needs.

Leadership is not an easy, comfortable place. When you lead — when you are a parent, a boss, or the leader of an organization — you have to put your feelings aside and make sure that the people you are responsible for get what they need.

What is Moses' response to the people complaining? Verse 25 says, *"So Moses cried out to the Lord for help."* Let's see how Moses faced this challenge.

1. He Cried Out in Desperation

Moses cried out in desperation. He has a challenge. He has to give people water. He has to make sure that these people get what they need, so here's what he does:

a) He turns to God and does not turn on the people. Moses does not get upset with the people. These people have just experienced a disappointing time in their lives. They end up being delivered and now they are dehydrated. Moses understands what they are going through. He says, 'God, I have done all that You have called me to do. You told me to get out of Egypt. You told me to cross the Red Sea, but You did not give me any details before I get to the Promised Land.'

That is what God will do to you. God will say to you, 'I want you to go to the Promised Land, but I am not going to tell you every single challenge you will face along the way.' Maybe God did not tell the Israelites about the challenges they would face because He knew that if some of the Hebrews knew they were going to be three days without water, many might have wanted to stay with Pharaoh.

Moses is doing what God says to do. He is not facing a challenge because he did wrong. He is facing a challenge because he did right. He did not turn on the people. He could have easily became mad at them, but as the leader, he had to understand that he could not act contrary to God's role for him as a deliverer. There is a reason God anointed him to lead them. God expected a different level of maturity from him in light of the challenges they were going to face. Moses did not turn on the people; he turned to God.

2. God Gave Him a Revelation

Moses called out to God, and God gave him a revelation. What kind of revelation did God give him? Verse 25: *"So Moses cried out to the Lord for help and the Lord showed him a piece of wood."* (Another translation says, God showed him a tree.) Then it says, *"Moses threw it into the water."*

A revelation is God revealing something that is not already seen or understood. As Moses faced this challenge, God said, 'Let Me show you something.'

a) God pointed out the tree.
b) God taught Moses about the tree.

c) God directed Moses in what to do with the tree.

When Moses was first shown the tree, he may have responded, 'What? A tree? This is a desert, God. You're showing me a tree — a dry tree in a desert? Did you not understand my prayer?' But God showed him the tree, and then He taught him about the tree, and then directed him as to what to do with tree.

When you see the word 'cry out,' in Hebrew, it simply means to point out or show. God pointed out the tree; He showed Moses something he was not paying attention to. God ended up teaching him or instructing him about the tree. The third thing God does is, He directs Moses in what to do. God says, 'I have to show you something you have not seen in this challenge that you are facing, because right now, it does not look like much; but wait until I get through with it. Moses, in the midst of all these people, I'm going to give you a revelation about your dry, desert situation. I have to point out something. I have to teach you about what I pointed out, and I have to direct you in what to do with it.'

"So Moses cried out to the Lord for help." That means Moses had come to a point where he could not do anything for himself. As a matter of fact, this is not the first time he has been here. He was just here at the Red Sea. Three days later, he runs into another crisis. If you're going to see the Red Sea part, you ought to have some confidence if you are the people or if you are the leader. But for some reason this water, this small spring, is giving us problems. God says, 'Hold up. Don't worry about it. I'm going to point out this

tree; I'm going to teach you about this tree; I'm going to tell you what to do with this tree.'

3. Moses Moved With Expectation

It's not enough to cry out in desperation. It's not enough just to get the revelation that God is giving. Now, Moses must take some action on what God has shown him. As we are reminded in our reading, God has not given him too much. It does not seem like a whole lot. However, Moses moved with expectation. Look at verse 25: *"Moses cried out to the Lord for help, and the Lord showed him a piece of wood."* It does not even say it is a whole tree. It does not even say it is alive. But that is what God showed him during this time. Here's what happened: *"Moses threw [the tree] into the water and this made the water good to drink."*

Moses moves with expectation as shown by his actions:

a) He moved with urgency. If he is going to face this challenge, he cannot hesitate. He has to move when God tells him to move. The Bible says in verse 25, *"The Lord showed him a piece of wood, and Moses threw it into the water."* He did not waste any time arguing with God about this wood. He is clearly hearing from God, and he's looking at something that does not make sense. But he moved urgently without argument and threw it into the water. He didn't pick up the tree and throw it beside the water. He didn't pick up the tree and start dancing with it. He took it and threw it into the water, because apparently the revelation God gave him said there is a particular place you must throw this wood. You have to do it now and you have to do it exactly like I told you. What does this challenge do for these people in this situation?

4. They Were Positioned for Restoration

This is the most important point: the Israelites were positioned for restoration. God is only going to get them close to what they need. He is only going to bring them to the situation. He is only going to change the situation by positioning them. They have responsibility if they are going to meet the challenge, finish the challenge, and make things better. How were they positioned for restoration?

a) They had to Trust that their leader heard from God. They are standing with Moses. 'Moses, we're thirsty. What are we going to drink? We haven't had anything to drink in three days.' Moses cried unto the Lord, 'Lord, You know I need some help down here?' God says, 'Moses, get that wood; pick it up and throw it in the water. It's all good.' Moses said, 'Alright you all; it's all good.' God allowed this situation where He says, 'I am not giving you another option. This is your only option. If you go forward, you are going to die of thirst. If you go backwards three days, you may not make it, and even when you get to the Red Sea, you cannot drink that water. It is sea salt water. Right now, you are in the only place that is an option.'

The Israelites had to trust that their leader had heard

from God. Why did they have to trust their leader? Because God did not do a three-way call when He gave directions to meet the challenge. God did not FaceTime or Skype or do a Google Chat with all of Israel. All they have is the person God put in their life who had a connection with God. Oftentimes God does not speak to the followers; He speaks to the leader. And the followers have to trust that the leader has heard from God.

I know you don't like that, but that's why we have so many marriages in trouble right now. We have men leading who aren't talking to the Leader. And then we have Eves following who want to tell Adam what to eat. We have a problem with "Follow the leader." That is the thing about vision: Sometimes people don't get what you get; they have to catch up with what you're getting. People will ask: Has this leader done anything that has not been trustworthy before? Do you have any evidence that this person has heard from God? Some of those Israelites did not like that, but that was all they had. Moses was who God had chosen. They had to trust that their leader had heard from God.

b) They had to Try by faith what they did not know by sight. God had already let Moses know that the water would be better. But the people would not know until they tasted it. We do not see anywhere in the scriptures that when he threw this wood in the water that the water changed color. We see nowhere in the scriptures where the water spoke and said, 'I'm good now.' We see nowhere in the scriptures that Moses tasted the water before he let everybody drink. They had to try by faith what they did not know by sight, because right now, God was doing something that was very uncomfortable for them.

God was saying, 'I want you to try again what just failed you not too long ago.' He said, 'I just did something to it. I know you can't look at it and see anything different. The only way you are going to end up knowing something is different is if you try it again. I'm not moving you from this place; I'm not giving you another option. If you're going to survive, the only way is for you to try something that disappointed you the first time. If you don't try it, you're going to die right where you are.' Their leader had heard from God, and the Israelites had to try by faith what they did not know by sight.

c) Their fate Turned from deadly to destiny. In verse 25, we read, *"Moses threw it into the water and that made the water good to drink."* God says to expect challenges in transition. Expect things to not be easy. Expect delays. Expect detours. Expect running out of what you need. Expect frustrating situations. In the midst of all that, here is the first thing you need to do, because right now, some of you are saying, that's the children of Israel. Well, guess what? You're a child of God. You have challenges in your life, right now. You have some things, that if God does not make a move, you'll be in a bad situation. I know there are some things, right now, in your life and you're saying, 'God, I have all this stuff coming up against me.' You cannot turn on the people who are near you, because that will only make your situation worse. When you end up arguing with people who cannot change your situation you can only make matters worse in your situation.

Do you have the faith of Moses? I do not know what you are facing. I do not know what your financial situation is. I do not know what physical dilemmas you are facing. But right now, we had better make sure we know how to face these challenges. Can I tell you how to face these challenges? Moses ended up crying out in desperation. Here's the reason you can't get delivered: Because you're not doing it like Moses did it. Moses did not go in a corner and cry out to God. Moses cried out to God in front of everybody. Moses said, 'My pride does not make a difference right now.'

You need to say, 'God, I have this situation, and right now, I don't care who is listening to me, I don't care who is looking at me, because they are not my audience any way.' The reason you cannot cry out in church in front of everybody is simply this: you are not desperate enough. The reason you might still be in debt is because you aren't desperate enough. I know you have jobs and you have stuff that's going on, but God will take you through some seasons where you're doing the best you can. But if you keep on pressing God — if you say, God I'm doing all that I can; I've obeyed you; I've done everything; I am tithing; I'm loving; I'm forgiving, and it is still bad — I dare you to lift your hands and say, 'Lord, I need You,' no matter who is watching.

Think about your situation and say to God, 'I am desperate.' Call on Him right now. He says, 'If you call, I will answer you.' I know what the problem is: you called and you did not get an answer. God wants to remind you, 'You have to get desperate enough to keep on calling.' The Bible says in Matthew 7:7, *"Ask, and it shall be given; seek, and ye shall find; knock, and the door shall be opened."* You have to understand that each word is a perpetual meaning. That means when I ask and I don't get it I have to keep on asking. God never said to beg Him; He says to ask Him. You ask somebody who loves you, but you beg somebody who does not care anything about you. You have asked your mama; you have asked the bank; you have asked your significant other; you have asked everybody else, but guess what? None of them have what you need. I dare you to ask the Father.

You have to ask, but then you have to seek. After you ask you have to go look and see whether or not it has shown up yet. If it hasn't shown up yet, you have to ask again, and then you go and look to see if it has shown up. And then if you don't see it, you have to knock. The church needs some desperate saints. We need people who will say, 'God, I need You to come through for me like never before. If You don't give me peace, I'm going to kill somebody. If You don't give me joy, I'm going to suffer from depression. If You don't give me what I need...' When you raise your hand it's like you are waving to God. "Here I am. I'm your child. I'm asking as a daughter. I'm asking as a son. I need Your healing." Ask. Be desperate. Cry out.

After you ask God and you get yourself out of the way, God gives a revelation. God shows you something you were not even thinking about. It's like the woman in the Bible when the prophet asked her, 'What do you have in your house?' Everything that she was looking at in her house was an answer to her problem; but it took a prophet to come and ask, "What's in your house?" You may be looking at something you have and you don't think it can meet your need. God is trying to tell you that He is about to show you that what you have been looking over is the answer to your problem. He says, 'You are going to need Me to touch your ordinary and make it extraordinary.'

The widow told the prophet, "I don't have anything but a little oil." The prophet said, "Don't worry about that. You just go and get some water pots and bring them in, and when I get through with them, they're going to be filled with oil, and the oil will keep flowing."

The problem is, you have been looking outside of yourself to look at everybody else who could help you. That is why God is shutting down everybody you used to depend on. He is asking you, 'Do you not know who you are? All you have to do is let Me put an anointing on your life.' All God used with the children of Israel was a raggedy old tree, but by the time Moses picked it up and threw it in the water a miracle took place. Sometimes, miracles happen, not because of who we are, but because of what God has done. Sometimes, miracles happen because of the anointing God has placed on our lives.

You may not understand what an anointing is. It is not a deep word. It means that God says,' I want to do something great with your life. I want to see if you can obey Me. I want to see if you can trust Me. I know right now you don't have a lot that you are working with, but when I get through putting My hands on you you'll go places you have never been before; you'll do things you have never done before. You'll marvel not only at yourself, but other people will marvel at you.'

God gave Moses a revelation and then directed him on how to carry it out. Moses moved with expectation. He moved as though God had already done it. Let me ask you this question: What has God told you to do and you're still asking Him, how? What has God told you to do and you're still asking Him, why?

Moses moved with expectation. When God speaks to you, do you expect Him to do the miraculous? That's His question. Why ask of Me and not do what I say? Because it does not make sense to you? Nothing in your life makes sense. You being alive does not make sense. He moved with urgency. He threw it in the right place.

They had tasted the water before, and it was the place where they had experienced disappointment; but God said to go back to that same place and try it again. Do you have a 'try it again' spirit? God says, 'I'm going to send you back to the same spot. I am not giving you any more options. I'm going to tell you to do it again because this time victory will replace your failure. Do you have courage enough? Do you have too much pride to go back and try again what failed you the last time? Can you deal with your friends and your family members calling you stupid because God told you to try it again?'

Perhaps someone reading this has already filed their divorce papers. You're admit on going through with it, but God says, 'Go try working on the relationship again.'

Because the Israelites tried it again, they were positioned for restoration. Why? God changed all their circumstances, but it would do no good if they did not do their part. God is only going to give you an opportunity; you have to show up. Quit expecting God to do it all. It is not going to happen. You have to be prepared for the opportunity. You have to be dressed for the opportunity. You need to be studying for what you have been praying about because when that opportunity comes, God wants you prepared. One of the worst things in life is to miss an opportunity that came your way because you took it lightly.

The Israelites' fate turned from deadly to destiny, because before the tree, there was bitterness, but after the tree, there was sweetness. Before the tree, they were frustrated, but after the tree, they were fascinated. Before the tree, they were empty, but after the tree, they were fulfilled. Before the tree, they were on the road to death, but after the tree, they were on the highway to new life. Before the tree, they had a bad outlook, but after the tree, they had a new perspective.

Some of you think I'm still talking about this tree. No, that was only a set-up for a New Testament church. I am talking about my life and your life before we recognized the tree that Christ was on. God had to introduce a tree into a bad world with a bad spirit. Before the tree, I had bitterness in my life; but after I had a taste of the tree, there was some sweetness in my life. The Bible says in Psalm 34:8, *"O taste and see that the Lord is good."* Before the tree, I was frustrated because I didn't know where I was going; after the tree, I knew to *"trust in the Lord with all my heart, and lean not to my own understanding. In all my ways acknowledge him and he shall direct my path."*

After the tree! Before the tree, I was empty; but after the tree, I've been filled with the Holy Ghost. I've been baptized in the Spirit. I've been bought with His Blood. I've been directed by Him and led by Him every single day. Before the tree, I was on my road to death, but, thank God, after the tree, I received new life. You still do not know what tree I am talking about?

At the cross, at the cross
where I first saw the light
and the burden of my heart rolled away.
It was there by faith
I received my sight,
and now I am happy all the day.

I'm happy because I'm saved. I'm happy because I know where I am going. I'm happy because I do not have to stay broke. I am happy because I do not have to stay depressed. I'm happy because I know who my Redeemer is. He is Jesus Christ.

When you get to the water, Jesus is not going to force you to drink. That's what that bitterness is in your mouth. God said, I need to get that taste out of your mouth. You need to quit having excuses about what happened last time you tried this. Take another drink.

"Then Moses led the people of Israel away from the Red Sea, and they moved out into the desert of Shur. They traveled in this desert for three days without finding any water. When they came to the oasis of Marah, the water was too bitter to drink. So they called the place Marah (which means "bitter").

Then the people complained and turned against Moses. "What are we going to drink?" they demanded. So Moses cried out to the LORD for help, and the LORD showed him a piece of wood. Moses threw it into the water, and this made the water good to drink.

It was there at Marah that the LORD set before them the following decree as a standard to test their faithfulness to him."

Exodus 15:22-25 (NLT)

Focus Verse: Verse 25: "So Moses cried out unto the Lord for help and the Lord showed him a piece of wood."

3

Expect a Character Check When You're in Transition

What's your character like?

As a matter of review, let us reflect on what we have already discovered about transition as we look into the lives of the Israelites. One of the first things we must expect in transition is, we have to go through some changes. Change is both exciting and scary at the same time. It is necessary. Going through changes is necessary when we are transitioning in our lives to the place where God has designed for us. We also discovered that like the Israelites there are four things we need to know that will help us navigate through some changes that we must expect in transition. These four things are:

1) We need to know what we must leave.
2) We need to know where we must go.

3) We need to know what we must experience.
4) We need to know how to keep the right perspective.

As we continued in our journey with the Israelites, we learned that we also must expect some challenges in transition. When you have changes there will also be some challenges that you will face. As the leader, Moses faced some challenges, but his response determined what position the followers would be in. First, Moses cried out in desperation. Then, God gave him a revelation. Third, Moses moved with expectation. Fourth, the children of Israel were positioned for restoration. Moses, by his leadership, his decision, and his listening to God, put the people of Israel in a good position. They have their water. They are ready to continue their journey to their destiny.

Not only will we face changes and challenges, but we also should expect a character check. When we are in transition, God says, 'I'm taking you somewhere, but I need to know what kind of character you have before you get to where you're going.' In other words, God will give us a destination, but we have to develop the character before we arrive. Have you ever seen someone get something but their character could not keep them in the place where God opened up the door for them? The Bible says in Proverbs 18:16, *"A man's gift will make room for him."*, but your character can get you kicked out of the room. God says, 'I'm sending you to the Promised Land, but I need to make sure you develop your character along the journey.' You want to get to the Promised Land, but God is trying to develop your character, and as your character is being developed, you're getting frustrated because character development sometimes brings frustration with it.

Now we have some background knowledge to help us understand how we came to this place. Moses led the children of Israel out of Egypt. God delivered them out of Pharaoh's hands, and they crossed the Red Sea. Pharaoh's army drowned in the Red Sea. They end up writing a song about all that God had done as recorded in Exodus 15:1-21. They celebrated. God told them, you can't stay here, so they ended up leaving on a three-day journey into the desert of Shur, but they were unsure of what would transpire in the desert. After traveling for three days, they ran out of water and God performed a miracle by Moses casting a tree into a bitter spring. The water then became sweet and the people were able to quench their thirst. The people celebrated. They now have what they need. But guess what? They are not at the end of their journey. They are still in transition. At this point, God has to stop them and say, 'Before you get to the Promised Land, I need to make sure I check your character because when you're going through challenges and changes you're showing me your character.'

Don't judge the children of Israel because when some of us go through changes and challenges we act out every now and then. When you're going through challenges, you get to see what's really in you. When you go through those changes, God says, 'Character is what I'm really after. I need to see where your character is.' Let's look at how the children of Israel responded during this character check. When God takes us through a character check, there are three things we should expect. First, let us see where we are.

The children of Israel had just had the sweet water and so now they are restored; now they are excited; now they are happy again. That is why you cannot depend on happiness, because to be happy something has to happen in your life. Something happened when they did not have any water: they were sad and mad. Then, they have water and now they are happy. You can't depend on happiness. That's why, as a Christian, you had better have joy. When you have joy it does not matter what happens because you recognize it's not what you have, it's who has you. And whenever you know who has you, you can be joyful because the joy of the Lord is your strength. With happiness, you're strong one day and weak the next. With joy, you have strength because your strength comes from the Lord, as He is the one who is your Sustainer and Provider.

How can you not be excited when you think about Jesus? How can you not get excited when you think about where He brought you from? How can you not get excited when you are in a relationship with somebody you know you don't deserve to be with? Even that by itself ought to make you happy. Look at all the things God has brought you through. Stop a minute and shout: 'I'm joyous right now!' You are going to be schizophrenic if you depend on happiness. Happiness is dependent on circumstances; but joy is dependent on relationship. What is your relationship like? If you check out your relationship with God, every now and then spiritual amnesia will rise up and you'll forget that God is still good. May I ask you something? Do you have joy on the inside?

God says, 'I need to make sure that before you get to the Promised Land you have the right character.' There are three things that God does during a character check. The first thing is, He answers a question for us:

1. Why Does God Provide Commands?

When God is doing a character check, He tells us why He is providing commands in our life. Look at verse 25: *"So Moses cried unto the Lord for help and the Lord showed him a piece of wood. Moses threw it into the water and this made the water good to drink. It was there at Marah that the Lord set before them the following decree as a standard to test their faithfulness to him."*

God says, 'I just blessed you all in a major way. As a matter of fact, I've opened up several doors and delivered you. It didn't take you but three days to turn on Moses. I just did a miracle in your life, but what I am recognizing with you now, by the way you are all acting, is that I need to set some boundaries for you all. I need to give some commands. I need to give some structure and have some order, and I have to do it right now while you're celebrating your breakthrough. I have to lay some ground rules so I can make sure you understand how to navigate through the rest of your desert-like situation. I have to put some ordinances in place.'

Here's why God provides commands:

a) They provide Limits for the people's lives. God says, 'Israel, you're all just coming fresh out of bondage. You have been living by the rules of an oppressive system. You've been on lock-down for over 400 years. What I have to do right now is tell you what My rules are as opposed to the rules you just came out from. I have rules to help you, not to hinder you. I have to set some boundaries so we can understand each other, so that we can understand where the limitations are and how far you can go and how far you don't need to go.'

b) They provide an Opportunity for the people to prove their loyalty to God. Here's what God is saying to His people: 'You know what, Israel? Right now, I'm providing commands for you. I'm setting the stage. I'm laying out ordinances. I'm setting out decrees. I'm making sure you understand that there is a wilderness manual. There is a relationship manual; when you are in a relationship with me, there are some boundaries you must observe and some freedoms that you have. There are some benefits and some consequences. You cannot be in relationship with Me any kind of way. I also want to provide an opportunity for you all to make sure that I understand what level of loyalty you have towards Me. In verse 25 it states, *"It was there at Marah that the Lord set before them the following decree as a standard to test their faithfulness to him."*

God says, 'I have to set My standards, because if you are not careful, you're going to go into the Promised Land with Pharaoh's standards. Your standards have to change if you are going to go where I am trying to tell you to go. You have been living with low and misinformed standards which caused bondage. If you're going to be blessed in the Promised

Land, you have to make sure you raise your standards. God's standards provide an opportunity for the people to prove their loyalty to God.

I remember seeing a cartoon that has two brothers. There is a fence that has two boards on it. On that fence is written God's commands. One brother is standing by the fence. The brother who is getting ready to jump over the fence is saying, 'I hate being confined by this fence.' But then when you look at it, the brother who's standing says, 'Wait! It's not a fence. It's a guard rail.' Let me explain: One brother has God's commands. He has the Word of God, yet he says, 'Oh, I'm so sick of this. All I read in the Bible is what I can't do.' The brother who's standing says, 'That is not no fence. It's a guard rail. God is trying to protect you from jumping over and killing yourself.'

God is telling Israel, 'I have to set some guard rails. What you are calling a fence is really a guard rail to protect you. Because I am your Father, My job is to set boundaries in your life. You need to know where and when not to do certain things.' We need to know why God provides commands.

2. There Are Some Questions About Their Character

Israel needed to know, first of all, why God is providing these commands. Secondly, God wants to get the right response from Israel so there are some questions He has to ask about their character.

He says, 'I have to ask the right questions of you because I want to see where your head is; I want to see where your heart is. I want to see if you can be loyal to Me on your own. I want to see if you view me as your best option. Let Me put forth some questions to you and about you:'

a) Can you pay attention? What do you mean by that? Let's look at verses 25-26: *"It was there that the Lord set before them the following decree as a standard to test their faithfulness to him. He said, If you will listen carefully to the voice of the Lord your God."* In other words, God says, 'I need to know: Will you listen to Me? Will you pay attention?' When you see this word, 'listen' or 'attention,' in the King James, it may say 'hearken.' Will they hearken unto the voice of the Lord? Hearken means to hear with attention or with interest. God says, 'I am about to talk to you, I am about to give you some directions, I am about to speak into your life, but the first thing I need to know is: when I start talking to you, are you going to pay attention like it interests you? If I, who am God, am speaking to you, Israelites, and you are just half listening, that will say a lot about your character. That will say a lot about how you see Me. Can you pay attention? Or do you have spiritual amnesia? Can you focus long enough to hear what I am saying to you? Are you listening with interest?'

b) Can you put into practice what you have been told? It's one thing for you to hear what I said; it's another thing for you to put into practice what I have told you to do. God says, 'I don't really have to ask you too many other questions. Here's what I have to check out: Can you put into practice what you have just been told?' The words or phrase used here means to hearken diligently. Diligently means speedily or with haste. In other words, when I tell you something, how fast will you respond? Will you respond speedily? Will you respond hastily? Will you respond at the very sound of My voice?

The Bible says, *"My sheep know My voice and another they will not follow."* 'You're going to respond to somebody quickly. I just want to know, will you respond to Me fast? Can you put into practice what I told you? Can you respond diligently? Speedily? Hastily? I don't want you just to respond fast; here's how I want you to respond: I want you to do what I say correctly. I want you to do it right because My eyes are on you. And not only are My eyes on you, other people's eyes are on you. Therefore, the question of the day is: Whose eyes do you want to look the best in? See, everybody has their eyes on you.'

This is what God is asking: Can you pay attention, and can you quickly put into practice what I have told you and in the way I told you because you want to be pleasing in My eyesight?

3. What Kind of Consequences God Will Deliver

God says, 'I am going to tell you why I provide commands, and then, I am also going to ask you some questions because I want to see your character. Now, if I get the right response out of you, there's a promise on what I will deliver to you.' What kind of consequences will God deliver? God says there are consequences to your actions. Let's look at verse 26: *"If you will...then I will."* God is saying, 'You are a partner in what happens to you next in your life. You are the other part of the equation. If you will...then I will. But that also means this: If you won't ... then I won't.' God says, 'I don't want you to blame anything on Me or the devil in your next season because what's about to be delivered to you is based on what you choose to do.'

You're going to have challenges from the devil, you're going to have things to go through. But this one's on you. You have personal responsibility where you cannot blame anybody else for the choices you make. You cannot blame your ancestors for what they didn't do for you. You cannot blame your daddy for letting you get locked up with Pharaoh. You can blame anyone you want to, but it does not matter now what happened before you crossed the Red Sea. What matters now is, what will you do on the other side of the Red Sea? He's saying to the Israelites: This is not about your past; this is about your future. Everything in your past did happen, but you get to decide in some way what happens in your future.

This is personal responsibility. What kind of consequences will God deliver into your life? Here are two things God promises He will do: First He says, He will protect them. God says, 'If you listen to My commands and do what I tell you to do, and your character looks good, I will show you My character: I will protect you.' Let's look at verse 26: *"If you will listen carefully to the voice of the Lord your*

God and do what is right in His sight..." Not because other people said it's okay. *"Obeying His commands and keeping all..."* God says this is no half-way thing. I want you to be clear on what I am asking of you in this next season of your life. You want a promised land, but can you obey in the desert? The Word continues: "*...all His decrees, then I will not make you suffer any of the diseases I sent on the Egyptians."*

God says, 'You all saw what happened to Pharaoh, right?'

'Yes, we saw it, Lord.'

'If you act like Pharaoh, you're going to get Pharaoh's consequences.'

You don't have to be a fool to experience fool's consequences. We're always saying, 'God won't put sickness on me.' You had better go and read your Bible. God will kill you as punishment for sin. Oh, yes, He will.

First Corinthians 10:13 says He'll never put on us more than we can bear. But, I bet you He will. Your consequences come from the things you do. You say that's Scripture. Yes, but you have to look at that Scripture in context. We recognized earlier in this study that there were some things Moses could not bear by himself. How do I know that? Because it says, *"He cried out in desperation."* He said, 'God, there is nothing else I can do about this situation.' When they arrived to the Red Sea, Moses did not know what to do. God had to let him know, 'You have more on you than you can bear. The reason I put it on you now is simply because I do not want you depending on you in this next situation. I want you depending on Me in this next situation. You've done all that you can do, now stand back and watch Me work.'

God says, 'I want to protect you from Me. If you obey, I'm going to keep Me off of you. That sounds like a real daddy. If you obey, I'm not going to let anything happen to you like what happened to the Egyptians.' God is like my daddy because my daddy used to discipline one of us and say, 'Now that's going to be you.' God says, 'If you act right, Israel, I'm going to protect you from some stuff that does not have to happen to you.'

The second thing is, God will become their personal physician. Look at verse 26: *"If you will listen carefully to the voice of the Lord your God and do what is right in His sight obeying His commands and keeping all His decrees, then I will not make you suffer any of the diseases I sent on the Egyptians."*

Notice who sent them: God did. This wasn't the devil's work. God sent it their way. God is very clear. He is not deceived, but He opened the door anyway. Disobedience opens the door where curses can walk in. God is saying, 'I am not sending disease that way; I am removing my covering from over you Egyptians. Now My wrath has to show up because My covering, My mercy, the door has been opened and now anything can walk in.' He says, 'I will protect you, Israel. I will become your personal physician.'

Verse 26 goes on to say: *"...for I am the Lord who heals you."* He is saying, 'I don't want you to get Me confused with what My role in your life is as Father. My role is not to kill you. My role is not to manipulate you. My role is not to bring you unnecessary pain unless it helps you. Understand who I am.' *"I am the Lord who heals you."*

This is God beginning to introduce Himself; He is showing them His character, so they can end up having better character. This is a side of God they had never seen. God says, 'I am Jehovah Rophi: the Lord who heals you. You don't need an HMO or a PPO. All you need is an O—obedience. You don't have any insurance, but when you end up obeying, guess what? I will personally be the God who heals you.'

Notice what He does not say He will be: He will not be the God who treats them, because God does not deal with symptoms. He says, 'I am the master healer. I heal; I do not treat.' Secondly, He is saying: 'I am not learning how to heal you; I am healing.' There is a difference between trying to be a healer and being healing. He says, *"I am the Lord who heals you."* In other words, His function for His people is to bring healing to the Israelites. He says, 'How do you know I am the Lord who heals you? Because just this day, you were thirsty and had bitter water, did you not?'

'Yes, Lord, we had bitter water. It was nasty water. We couldn't drink that water. The water was sick.'

'Yes, it was sick. I told Moses to get a piece of wood and throw it into the water, and guess what? Is the water sweet?'

'Yes, it became sweet water. We thank You for the Aquafina. We thank You, right now, Lord. We praise You, right now.'

'Just like that water was sick, Israel, and I put wood in the water and now you are able to drink the water that I healed, every time you end up in a situation where you feel sick, where you feel broken, where you feel like you are about to die, remember what I did when you had some sick water on your hands. If I can heal sick water, what do you think I am going to do with your sick life?'

God says He will protect them; He will be their personal physician, their personal Rophi. Rophi means:

a) To sew together. If He is bringing healing, then God says, 'I have to become the God of stitches because there is something in your life that has caused an open wound. And My job to Israel now is to sew you back together.' It also means:
b) To mend; to mend what was broken.
c) To restore. Often, when we read in the Bible where God has restored something, it means that a bone has popped out of socket and God snaps and resets it so it can be restored and begin the healing process to get back to where it needs to be. Sometimes God says, 'I have to cause you pain to get your healing straight.'

When I used to play football, I dislocated a finger once while trying to catch a punt. I was sitting there at the doctor's table in the hospital in pain. My finger is swollen. It is still swollen after almost twenty-something years. I'm sitting with the doctor and he's looking at me and talking to me.

"Does it hurt?"

"Yea, it hurts. Why are you wiggling my finger? Don't you see how crooked it is?"

He said, "I'll be back." He went and spoke with somebody else. When he came back, he put his hand on my shoulders and started asking me some questions.

I'm like, "Yea, ... Ow, man! What are you doing?"

"I just had to reset your finger; I had to distract you first."

God is saying, 'Sometimes I have to distract you with conversation even while you're in pain; but don't worry about that as I have to cause you pain to restore you. Don't think the pain is meant to kill you; it is meant to heal you.' Sometimes you know you're getting healing because it starts hurting. Sometimes it hurts before it gets better. 'You can't be restored, Israel, unless you've lost something. But before you lose anything else in your life, Israel, know I am already in the restoring business. Then as you are losing stuff, Israel, I am walking behind you with what I am going to replace it with because that's who I am: The God who restores.'

To sew together. To mend. To restore. The fourth meaning is:

d) To heal. It means to heal physically and emotionally. *"I am the Lord who heals."*

This conversation we're having is because someone reading this is saying, 'You know what, God, I know you're taking me somewhere, but I am frustrated I'm not there yet. Why? What's going on right now?'

God says, 'I'm getting your character in check.'

'But, God, I'm good. I've done this.'

Guess what? Where you're going you have to take it to another level.

God is saying, you cannot enter into the next season thinking the work habits that you have in this season are good enough. You came into your next season thinking the prayer life you had in your last season was good enough. You have to understand that God has to provide some commands in our life. God has to set some boundaries in your life. Do you thank God for some boundaries He's set in your life? Do you thank God that what you were calling a fence was really a guard rail? You did not recognize it until God allowed you to walk away from it, because somebody ended up talking you down from jumping over.

Let me break it down for you. You saw that person who you thought you just had to have walking in the mall the other day, and you said, 'Oh, thank God, there was a guard rail and not a fence, because, God, You protected me from messing up my life by hanging with them. Thank You for the guard rails in my life.'

There is something you've been praying about; there's something you've been wanting to have and God won't let you have it but everybody else around you is getting everything they want. Have you ever prayed and God answered all your prayers, but He gave your answers to your friends? They are getting stuff they did not even ask God for. And here you are still struggling, and you're checking, and God says, 'Don't worry about it. I'm protecting you from something.' The frustrating thing about God is, you never know what He is protecting you from until you pass by it. Sometimes you never know what He is protecting you from at all. But that does not matter. Allow me to tell you why you're still mad at God: It is because there are some people you know who aren't really trying to be as holy as you are, who aren't trying to do right as you are, who aren't trying to manage their money as you are, and, yet, they go out and do anything they want. They never get caught. But you go out just one time and try. Can you identify with what I am saying here?

When I was growing up and our parents wouldn't let us do something, we would complain, saying, 'Well, So-and-So's daddy...' My daddy would let us know. 'You are not So-and-So's child; you're my child.' You, dear Christian, are God's child. And God does not let His kids just do anything. God does not want His kids walking out looking any kind of way. God does not want His kids just growing up any kind of way. God will check His kids because He loves His kids.

Hebrews 12 says if your 'Father, God, does not discipline you, you're like a bastard child.' That is not a curse word. A bastard child is one who has no daddy. I thank God that He stopped me when I was going to do some wrong, because God says, 'You are My child, and I have plans for you.' There are some things you cannot do. There are some places you cannot go. I know you're saying there are places I used to go to that I don't go to anymore. God stopped you from going to those places that you wanted to go to and sometimes you went to those places anyway, but by the time you arrived there, their desire was gone.

Somebody you wanted, God won't even let you love them like you wanted to. You wanted to get that love back, but God said, 'I am drying it up right now. I am taking it out of your system because I don't want you standing over something that should have been buried a long time ago.'

Boundaries. There are some thoughts that cross my mind that if you even knew what was going on in my head sometimes, you'd end up saying, "Are you sure you're a preacher?" I thank God that even though I have crazy thoughts in my head, God will not let me do everything I am thinking because if I did everything I thought somebody would be dead. If it wasn't for the grace of God setting boundaries in my life, I would have done some terrible things. We all should thank God for His grace and His mercy.

You had better be glad that some of the people you hang around are saved because if you knew us before we were saved, we would have been different people. I try to think or act like I'm saved every day, but unfortunately I don't succeed. Every now and then, I still have a little cursing in me, but Jesus built a fence all around my mind, around my mouth, around everything. Thank God for His boundaries. Thank God for His commands. Thank God His words are not meant to kill; they are meant to heal.

Do you thank God that He knows how to check our character? He says, can you pay attention when I call on you? When I tell you to do something I don't want you procrastinating. If you've been hurt by someone and I tell you to go and forgive that person, how long is it going to take you? Do you have to go through all of what you feel and what happened to you and what it did? Or do I have to show you another example of putting My Son on the cross? Even though He did not do anything wrong, He was able to look back at them and say, "Father, forgive them for they know not what they do."

God is saying, 'Can you practice what you've been told? Can you run the risk of disappointing people to please God? Can you lose the job because you'd lose your integrity if you took it? Can you say 'no' to the relationship because it will stunt and stall your purpose?' God says, 'Who do you want to please? Me or people?' God says, 'You had better learn how to please Me and let them be mad at you, because if I'm mad at you and they are happy with you, both of you are going to be highly upset.'

Finally, we see the consequences. God says, if you obey Me and you move when I tell you to move, and you do what I call you to do, and you have the right kind of character, notice what you are going to get from Me: you will receive healing.'

The reason you keep walking around depressed is because you keep looking at what happened to you. The Bible says, "Look to the hills from whence cometh my help." How do I do that? You have to look and say, 'This did happen. But guess what? He has more in store for me.' If that does not help you in looking forward, look backwards and see where you came from. Be crazy enough to look over your shoulder and see where God has brought you from. Look at what He's saved you from. Look at what He kept you from. Look at what He brought you out of. What has happened is, you became too comfortable with God. You are too cool pretending you can't even remember where He has brought you from because you think that only deserves one shout. You had better get your mind together. Every time I think about His goodness, I get excited about where

He brought me from.

Can you say, 'I looked over my life and all I can say is if it wasn't for the grace of God I would have died right there? I would have gone crazy right there? In fact, I did become crazy-crazy right there. I was dead right there. My finances were dead. My relationships were dead. My self-esteem was dead. My faith was dead. But God...'

Can you still obey even though it hurts? Can you keep on loving even though it hurts? Can you keep on reading the Scriptures even though it hurts? God says, "I am the God that heals thee. I am the God that restores thee." You lost some stuff because God said you need some new stuff in your next season. You ought to put your hands together and say, 'God, thank You for what You are bringing My way. And if it's not physical, first, bring me more joy, bring me more peace, bring me more anointing so I can do more of Your will for You, so I can touch more lives for You, so I can lead more people to You.'

"I am the Lord who healeth thee." I AM. Stop looking for the person who hurt you to heal you. If they could have done that, they would have done that already. Some of you have dead people holding you hostage. You're held hostage by a dead beat daddy. You're held hostage by a dead beat mama, a dead beat cousin, or a dead beat friend. How long are you going to let a dead person have access to the keys to your life? It's a character check.

God is really asking: How quick can you get over stuff? We're not talking about forgetting what happened. 'I'll forgive and forget.' No, you don't forget. Forgetting means you do not have any wisdom, because if you hit me three times I know how to duck on the fourth. I am not forgetting anything. To forget means I'm not going to treat you like I did before. I'm going to treat you like it never happened because what you do I cannot control, but I can control what I do to you. It takes more strength for me not to harm you. It takes more strength for me not to expose you. God has put some of you in a situation where all your life you were the disadvantaged one. Now, God has revealed to you some things about people. Now the people who mistreated you are at a disadvantage. What God is saying right now is, 'I want to see how you handle it when you have the advantage.' It's a character check when you have the power. I already know how you react when you have been abused; nobody blames the victim too much. But what do you do when you're the one in control? What kind of character do you have? You can choose to be like the person who messed over you. That's the danger of unforgiveness. You end up becoming what you despise. What are you going to do?

God has a Promised Land waiting on you. What kind of character are you going to have when you arrive? It's not always about the destination; it's about the journey. You may have been hurt over and over and you keep asking God, 'When? When am I going to stop hurting?' The answer is, when you get better character. When you stop responding out of your flesh.

You say, 'Why do I have to go through so much?'

God says, 'Because I have so much waiting on you. This process is painful, but I'm building character in you right now.'

"Then Moses led the people of Israel away from the Red Sea, and they moved out into the desert of Shur. They traveled in this desert for three days without finding any water. When they came to the oasis of Marah, the water was too bitter to drink. So they called the place Marah (which means "bitter").

Then the people complained and turned against Moses. "What are we going to drink?" they demanded. So Moses cried out to the LORD for help, and the LORD showed him a piece of wood. Moses threw it into the water, and this made the water good to drink.

It was there at Marah that the LORD set before them the following decree as a standard to test their faithfulness to him. He said, "If you will listen carefully to the voice of the LORD your God and do what is right in his sight, obeying his commands and keeping all his decrees, then I will not make you suffer any of the diseases I sent on the Egyptians; for I am the LORD who heals you."

Exodus 15:22-26 (NLT)

Focus Verse: Verse 25: "It was there at Marah that the Lord set before them the following decree as a standard to test their faithfulness to him.

4

Expect Code Compliance When You're in Transition

It has already been established that transition is necessary if we're going to achieve, if we're going to arrive, if we're going to fulfill everything that God desires for us to fulfill in our lives. So far, as we study the lives of the Israelites as they transition en route from Egypt on their way to the Promised Land, we've discovered three things already that God wanted them to expect when they were going through transition.

The first thing we understood was that they were to expect changes. The next thing we saw was that they needed to expect some challenges. Third, we saw that they needed to go through a character check. Now we see the fourth thing the Israelites need to expect is code compliance.

You may be wondering, how in the world did I get this out of these scriptures. Well, code compliance means the inspection of a property to make sure it is up to the standards of a city and that its codes have been obeyed fully so one can receive a certificate of occupancy. The inspector has to make sure that everything had been built and maintained according to the city's standards. Even though you buy a house or a building in a city, you don't buy the city. Since you don't buy the city, you have to go by the city's rules if you are going to stay in what you bought. One of the easiest ways to describe the need to expect code compliance in transition is what my church went through when we acquired a temporary building on 900 Polk Street.

Here's what's took place with us as we made the transition into our new building. These four things are things one can expect when one is in transition and where one needs code compliance:

1) Expect to Reposition. Here's what that means: We had to leave our current location and reposition ourselves in a temporary location — 900 Polk Street. We had planned to move in that June. However, we had to make sure that we were operating by faith. We knew that we had to reposition. We could not stay where we were if we were going to go where God wanted us to go. When we get to that transitional place, the second thing to expect is ...

2) Expect to find prepared Resources. We already expected God to have an abundance of resources available to us in our new transitional place, not just to be a blessing to us, but to be a further blessing to the people we have been called to serve. Do you expect God to do even greater things? By faith, we already know that God wants us to move from faith to faith and glory to glory, and we've mentioned how that God never moves you from one place unless He's already provided another place because God is moving us from just enough to more than enough. It isn't about us; it's about what we have been assigned to do. We expected before we even arrived over there that God was going to do great things. Do you believe God is going to do greater things in your transition? If we were going to end up occupying our transition building, then we needed to ...

3) Expect to Restructure. Before we could occupy the new building, we had to restructure some things. As a matter of fact, that building had to be restructured because it could not handle the church the way it was then. It had to be refitted and reconfigured because it is a prepared place for a prepared people. God cannot move a prepared people into an unprepared place. God is a God of timing in transition. He says, 'If the building is not ready then you are not ready, and there's some more things that I am working on before you can get in here.' The plane cannot land because there are some = things on the ground that needs to be moved out of the way. Some things had to be fixed before we could occupy the building. We could not move in because it had to go through a series of inspections, and some of those inspections do not take just one or two days. Some of those inspections may take one or two weeks. They had to test the building before it was approved and before we were allowed to move in. Because of this testing, it took us longer to move in. Why did it take longer to move in? Because we can expect to restructure before we go in.

If we are going to be in code compliance as we move into transition, there is a fourth thing we can expect:

4) Expect to Rest. This does not mean we are going to get over there and just chill. When you are in code compliance with the city and the codes, here's what you can do: you can rest well in your mind knowing that when you move in you will be safe. You can rest well in your mind knowing that when you move in you don't have to come back and correct something. You can rest assured knowing that when you come in you are already protected because the fire sprinkler is in place so if a fire breaks out you know the water is going to work. You know where the exits are. You know everything is in place, so you can rest peacefully.

Here's another thing we can do: We can worship in Spirit and in truth. How many of you know that when you are in a safe place you can just be yourself? You can get all the worry off your mind. You don't have to worry about what's taking place. Rest can come when you are in transition. And when you have code compliance, you can make sure that when you go into your transitional building, you can worship there in peace until you make your next move.

Now, let's transfer that into the lives of the Israelites. The Israelites needed to expect these four things as well as they make their journey to the Promised Land.

1. Expect to Reposition

Where did we get this from? It's right there in verse 27: *"After leaving Marah, the Israelites traveled on to the oasis of Elim..."*

God says, 'You all need to **expect to reposition.** Israelites, you cannot stay at Marah. Marah was a bitter place that I turned into a good place. You shouted. You became excited. You drank the water, but that is not all I have for you. I did a special thing, but you are going to have to leave that place where I worked a miracle. You are going to have to leave a place where I did something spectacular in your life. I don't want you to get so used to what I did yesterday that you think that's all I can do. Marah is not your destination. Marah is a layover. I don't want you falling in love with a layover. Understand that Marah did what Marah was supposed to do. I do not want you building any brick houses at Marah. Make sure you build a tent because you can just let Marah know, I'm excited about being here today, but tomorrow I have to go.'

In life, you need to make sure you get ready to move from that place, You have to move from a place where miracles took place, where commands were given, where character was tested, and where consequences will take place if you don't obey. If you are willing to obey, you're going to see God's good side, and you can expect to see His healing.

That's not all that will happen when you leave Marah...

2. Expect to Find Prepared Resources

"The Israelites traveled on to the oasis of Elim where they found twelve springs, and seventy palm trees..." Remember, it was a three-day journey just to get to Marah. It was about thirty miles, and now they have to transition to a new place they have

never been to. You have been to Marah; it took you three days to get there. Now, it is going to take you another day to get to the next spot. You have already been blessed in one place after a bad experience, but now you have to get up and move on to another place.

When you are reading about the children of Israel and their journey from Egypt all the way to the Promised Land, they did not just have two stops on their journey; they had fifty stops from Egypt all the way to the Promised Land. Fifty stops. Now here is the problem: all fifty stops were not God-ordained. Some of the stops were unnecessary stops. Some of the stops were because they were being disobedient towards God. They only had eleven days to travel; but it took them forty years to take that eleven days journey because they ended up stopping at places due to their bad behavior and their character flaws, so God allowed them to have grace in a place longer than they needed to. During that grace period—that forty-year period—some of them died.

When God has you to go somewhere make sure you obey quickly. Check your character. He says, 'When you leave Marah, I want you to have your expectations high. I don't want you leaving Marah with your head down. I want you to leave Marah having in the back of your mind what I just did when you departed Egypt. I want you to leave Marah remembering how Marah was when you showed up. Marah was not even a good place when you showed up; but I allowed you to stay being that you did not have any more options. No sooner than you arrived at this bitter place, it turned out to be a blessing as I made it a better place. You were excited about Marah. You didn't want to be at Marah, but when I went through the trials and transitions within Marah, you fell in love with it. Now I'm telling you to get ready to move from the place I made good; I do not want you to linger here any longer.'

Marah isn't your destination; it's just a layover en route to your transformation. God says, 'Now when you move to your new place expect to find prepared resources.'

The children of Israel are on a journey. God made a provision in a bad place. Now they are leaving the only resource they have in the desert. God says, 'Don't worry about it. When you get to where you're going, you'll recognize I already have you covered. This is movement from what you see by sight. You have to leave what you see to embrace what you can't see.' God says, 'I promise you that if you leave what you can see, what you can't see will be even better. I dare you to trust Me. If you leave what you see, what you are comfortable with, and what you are familiar with, by the time you get to what you can't see you'll recognize I already hooked you up before you showed up.'

Prepared resources. The word "prepare" or "provide" means to 'pro- / pre-see.' That means, God said, 'I have already pre-seen your needs, and I have already done inventory on what you're going to need when you leave this place. Don't worry about it; all I need for you to do is to keep walking. Just keep walking. If you keep walking, you're going to run into what I have already prepared for you.' He says, 'Expect to find prepared resources.' As the Israelites kept walking, one day later, they found three things: water, shade, and food. The scripture says, *"...where they found twelve springs, and seventy palm trees; they camped there beside the water."* There was water already prepared for them. It was just sitting and waiting on them. There was also shade which was welcomed because they had been in the heat of the desert; it was draining them and they were risking dehydration again. God said, 'Don't worry about it; I already have some palm trees waiting on you.' There were also dates in that particular part of the world so they were able to eat of the fruit of the dates. God had already provided for them water, shade, and food.

The water was in abundance, and this time God did not have to sweeten it; it was already sweet. They did not have to have any miracles where they were going. When they relocated, they had protection from the sun. So, He says, 'Expect to find prepared resources.' What kind of resources are we talking about? We're talking about twelve springs. These twelve springs, or wells, were natural wells. All the other wells they had to dig to get the water. These were naturally coming from another source and now they were bubbling up by themselves. All the Israelites had to do was to show up and drink. They did not have to come into this season digging wells and sweetening the water. All they had to do was show up and receive what God had already provided for them. The water was already there. God says, 'I want you to make sure that you turn up expecting to find prepared resources. I have you covered.' Expect to reposition. Expect to find prepared resources.

3. Expect to Restructure

God is saying: You have to reorganize before you partake in the resources I've already provided for you. As mentioned before, it's at least a million people. There are only twelve wells and seventy palm trees. How many of you know there will be some fighting and some pushing and some shoving if somebody does not get organized? God says, 'I can have the resources waiting on you, but you have to get in an organized fashion. You have to restructure your position if you're going to end up surviving off of what I have already provided for you. He says to reorganize before they partake of the prepared resources.

Remember in verse 27 it explains what they had found or what they stumbled upon. It says, *"They found twelve springs."* If you understand biblical numerology, twelve means a divine government; it means divine order; it means structure. God says, 'Right now you have to get structured because there are only twelve wells.' Before they went into Egyptian bondage, Jacob had twelve sons and from these came the twelve tribes of Israel. So God says, 'I want you to remember who you were before you went into bondage for four hundred years. You are still the twelve tribes of Israel. So right now, I want you to get into your tribes, because I do not want anybody fighting over a well as I have a well for every family that shows up. You don't have to fight their family for their well because I have a well for you.'

'If you're not getting restructured you're going to have disorganization, and where there is disorganization there is strife, anger, jealousy, and bitterness because there is no one in position to get what's theirs. They are just trying to get something and they don't realize what belongs to them. You have to remember who you are and Whose you are. You've been in bondage for a long time. I have prepared twelve springs all ready for you before you showed up, and now I'm telling you at this point in your life, you have to get reorganized so that you look and think about situations going forward.'

There were twelve springs, but then there were seventy palm trees. In verse 27 it says, *"they found twelve springs, and seventy palm trees."* The number seventy is a number that also means spiritual order carried out with divine power and fullness. A seven and ten together: seven is completion; ten is fullness. Seventy means it is completely full. It means whatever you need right now, you will have in abundance. You'll have more than enough. Not only that, but everything that you had before you came here I am about to give you more than what you need. I'm about to give you a full life because seventy was the amount of years—three score and ten—that a man was able to live. The reason I let you get to these seventy palm trees is to show you I don't plan on you dying before you get to where you're trying to go.

God says, 'Water is bubbling up from these wells; there won't be any work that you have to do. I know you are not accustom with this and you feel uncomfortable because you're used to digging wells for Pharaoh, but you are in a new season. You are in a new place. Now, I am about to bless you and pay you back for what you had to do when somebody didn't pay you what you were worth.' That is why you don't ever need to worry when people do you wrong because God will make it up. He'll end up moving you to another place. When someone does you wrong, say, 'That's alright. I have a God who already has something prepared for me. You all didn't treat me right back there, but I'm not going to get mad at you. I'm not going to curse you out because you don't supply my needs. My God shall supply all my needs.'

Do you know that God will make up for what other people mess up in your life? And God knows how to give you exceedingly abundantly far above all that you could ask or think.

Before the Israelites were in bondage, Jacob had twelve sons. These twelve sons had family members, and these family members, numbering seventy, all went into Egypt. They went through all kinds of hell under Egyptian bondage, but they multiplied and grew to almost two million by the time they came out of Egypt. God is saying, 'Do you know what? I have seventy palm trees because I want you to remember how this thing was started. I want you to remember the seventy who started because seventy also means a generation.' God is saying, 'When you look at these seventy palm trees one generation went into slavery, but another generation is about to come out of slavery and go into the Promised Land because I am a God who keeps His word.'

Twelve. Seventy. Let's talk about this prophetically and symbolically. We have to understand what is going to take place next with twelve and seventy in the story: Before they get into the Promised Land, God is going to divide up the land among all twelve tribes. God says, 'Before you all get to the Promised Land, I'm going to tell you what you each own. You're not even close yet, but let me tell you what belongs to you before you show up so that when you go in you won't have to fight over somebody else's things, and you can go in by faith knowing that you already have it. I want you to have it in your mind and in your heart before it's under your feet. I want you to trust My word that I already have a prepared place for you before you get to that place.' That's why we can say, don't wait until the battle is over; you can shout now.

Do you have faith that God says there is something He has for you already? I'm telling you what you have right now, but you're going to get it by faith. *'For we walk by faith and not by sight (2 Corinthians 5:7).''* Can you shout over some things you know God is about to do in your life? God has already made some promises. If you don't have the money, don't worry; the business is still yours. If you don't have the money, don't worry; the car is still yours. If you don't have the money, don't worry; it's already yours. Do you feel as though God is doing something, but it does not make sense to you how it's going to happen? God says, don't worry about it; it's by faith. It's on the way. It's already yours. It's already done.

We also see the number seventy because as the Children of Israel move forward, God says, 'Moses, you can't lead all these people by yourself. I need you to get seventy elders and put them over the people; I want you to make sure that they cover the people.' See, there were twelve tribes and then there were seventy elders. There were twelve wells and there were seventy palm trees. The last time I checked out a palm tree it towered over people. It provided a covering for them. God said to Moses, 'Make sure they have your spirit in them. You don't need someone who has the wrong spirit leading others.' God wanted elders who would protect the people, cover them, and provide food, nourishment, training, and development for them to get to where they need to go.

In the New Testament, we see the number twelve show up in the number of men Jesus called to be His disciples. These were not just ordinary disciples; they were apostles. Twelve means structure, order, or government. Jesus is setting up the government of God, God's Kingdom, on the earth. Now that those twelve have an apostolic anointing on their lives, the Kingdom of God is rising in place of the kingdom of the devil because a war is about to take place, and we will now see what God's Kingdom looks like on the earth again. God is not just coming; He's coming to take over.

After He sets up the twelve apostles, the next thing we see is that there were seventy disciples. These seventy disciples would go among the rest of the people. They would be connected to the twelve because the twelve would be their covering; the twelve would give them direction. The seventy isn't anything and the twelve isn't anything unless they get back to the source who is Jesus. The stream that made the wells happen and made the trees grow is nothing without the stream that made it flow. Do you know Jesus is your stream?

Now God says,

4. Expect to Rest

God tells the Israelites, 'In this next season, I want you to R-E-S-T. Rest. You've been through a lot. Rest. That does not mean it is over, but if God is telling them to rest that means there's a long journey ahead. God says, 'You can't end up going where I am taking you tired, confused, and broken down. You need time right now to rest from your travels, rest from your troubles, rest from your toiling. I've already provided for you the place where you can rest. All you have to do is rest at the Seventy Palm Desert Resort. Kick your feet up by the water and rest. Don't take your laptop. Don't take your iPhone. Don't take your iPad. Right now, all I want you to do is talk to Me and talk to each other and just rest.'

That's what's wrong with many of us. We'll stop cursing so much if we just get some rest. We'll stop looking cross-eyed at people if we just get some rest. We need to sit down somewhere and rest. Rest right now in peace so you will not have to rest in pieces. Expect to rest.

Right now you're saying, alright, I heard what to expect for code compliance for the church. That's cute. I heard what the Israelites need to do for their code compliance. That's wonderful, but what about me? How does that fit for me?

Right now, God is transitioning your life. God is saying, 'You've been at Marah too long.' You have become caught up with Marah for so long you are beginning to think there is nothing sweeter than Marah. You have become accustom to

Marah, but there is something better than Marah. God says, 'I am changing your mindset right now. I'm changing your attitude because I'm getting ready to uproot you from a place you have become comfortable in. You think those are the only miracles I can do? You think that's the best thing I can present you with? You think that's all I can do in your life? Don't worry about it. It is not about your education. You don't have to go to school for this one. All you have to do is obey what I have told you.'

We don't see Jesus' degrees on the cross. We only see His obedience on the cross and that makes all the difference. When you obey God, He will make up for what you don't have. He does not call those who are prepared; He prepares those who are called. It's time to leave. It's time to kiss them goodbye. It's time to wave bye-bye. It's time to prepare for your exit interview. It's time to get your things in order, because God is about to open a door you have never seen yet. God is getting ready to tell you to move and when He tells you to move, you'd better not hold on to what you have. You'd better let it go because God says, 'I have a prepared place for you if you can just take your eyes off of what you can see just for a moment and take a faith walk with Me.'

'I know what you're used to. I know what circles you're used to running in. I know what will end up holding you down and making you feel comfortable, but right now, I want to disturb your comfort zone. You don't even know why I am getting ready to say this, but I'm about to change something. And when I change it, I don't want you giving notice on Me. I don't want you getting upset with Me. I told you before I was going to do it that, I was going to restructure your life because there is something I have waiting on you.'

You are one day away from twelve springs and seventy palm trees. When you crossed the Red Sea and were dying of thirst for three days, God performed a miracle and saved you. After three days, He said, 'Alright, that's cool. I just wanted to see how you were going to act because I already have your springs waiting on you. I just wanted to see how you were going to handle it yesterday.'

You may be one prayer away from the greatest experience in your life. You may be one breakthrough away from God giving you what you need to make your next transition. You are one application away from the job of your dreams. You're one hello away from meeting the love of your life. Are you getting excited about what God is about to do in your life? Then say, 'God, I thank You. Even though I cannot see it, I'm going to thank You that I am a lot closer than I thought I was.' God is not going to get you this far and leave you. That's why your money is drying up: because you're in transition. That's why your friends are getting low: because you're in transition. There are enough wells out there for everybody, and God is about to give you what belongs to you.

You shouldn't want somebody else's life or things they have. You should want what God has for you. What God has for you is for you and nobody else. Have you been praying about some changes? Have you been praying about a breakthrough? I dare you right now to lift up both your hands and say, 'Have Your way. Rain down on me right now.

Open up the windows of Heaven and pour out a blessing.' A delay is not a denial. Get that worry off of you. Get that depression off of you. Get that frustration off of you. He's going to make up for the deficit. If you'll just obey Him, He'll give you what you can't do on your own.

God is trying to make you like a palm tree. It doesn't matter what's going on around a palm tree. The palm tree does not base its existence on what it sees. It bases its existence on what it cannot see. It will dig to find its water source. And it just does not exist in the desert; it flourishes in the desert. God says I'm going to make you flourish around everybody else who's dry, who's broken, who's busted and disgusted. You're going to be a palm tree. You might say, I'm lonely.' God is saying, 'I have to isolate you out here in the desert by yourself so that you can learn how to dig and depend on Me and quit depending on others because I'm getting ready to elevate you.'

Another thing about a palm tree is, if you cut it, it won't die. If you wound it, it won't die because its existence is not based on what happens externally. Its life is on the inside. It has its healing resource on the inside that says, 'No matter what you do to my external, I'm still going to live.' "*Greater is He who is in you than he who is in the world.*" That's why others lied on you, you didn't kill yourself even though you thought about it. That's why when others dogged you and left you, you're still standing strong.

The palm tree digs its roots into the ground because it's looking for something to hold on to. It knows that a wind and a storm are coming, and no matter how strong the wind the palm tree just bends. Palm trees are designed to grow straight up so it just fights back. When the wind blows it to one side, the palm tree says, 'I can't stay like this because I was born to stand,' and it straightens back up. The storms of financial problems, the storms of relational problems, the storms of insecurity have taken their best shots at you, but you can look around and say, 'I'm still standing.'

The other thing about a palm tree is its branches. The leaves of the palm tree represent victory. When you wave a palm tree leaf, it's representative of when the Lord Jesus was coming into Jerusalem on the donkey. "Hosanna! Hosanna in the highest." That means Jesus has entered into your life. It means Jesus is about to do something in your life that you have never seen before. Can you wave your hand like a palm tree leaf and say, 'Devil, you thought you had me, but I still have the victory'?

You have to be in code compliance. I told you that the city has to approve you before you move in. You don't understand what has been going on the whole time with your life? The city I am talking about is Heaven. The general contractor is Jesus, and He's doing an inspection because your body is the Temple of the Holy Ghost. And Jesus says, 'If you want this body to move into Heaven, it has to be reconstructed. It has to go either through the Rapture or through the grave.' When we are transitioned we don't know what the transition will be like, but we know in the twinkling of an eye we shall look like Him. And only then will you be able to have your Certificate of Occupancy. Only then will you be able to march into Heaven.

The only thing that can grant you access is, believing that Jesus lived, that Jesus died, and that Jesus rose again, and then He will move into your temple.

"Then Moses led the people of Israel away from the Red Sea, and they moved out into the desert of Shur. They traveled in this desert for three days without finding any water. When they came to the oasis of Marah, the water was too bitter to drink. So they called the place Marah (which means "bitter").

Then the people complained and turned against Moses. "What are we going to drink?" they demanded. So Moses cried out to the Lord for help, and the Lord showed him a piece of wood. Moses threw it into the water, and this made the water good to drink.

It was there at Marah that the Lord set before them the following decree as a standard to test their faithfulness to him. He said, "If you will listen carefully to the voice of the Lord your God and do what is right in his sight, obeying his commands and keeping all his decrees, then I will not make you suffer any of the diseases I sent on the Egyptians; for I am the Lord who heals you."

After leaving Marah, the Israelites traveled on to the oasis of Elim, where they found twelve springs and seventy palm trees. They camped there beside the water."

Exodus 15:22-27 (NLT)

5

Expect Complaining When You're in Transition

God does not want us to be shocked when certain things take place when we are transitioning in our lives—whether we're transitioning as a church, as a company, as a family, or as an individual. Whatever it is that God is transitioning you in—be it in thought, habit, location, or relationship—here are changes that you must go through. After you go through changes, there are challenges, character checks, and code compliance. As we continue our journey with the Israelites, we realize we also must expect complaining in transition. Expect it! If it's not from you, then expect it from the people who are connected to you. When changes are taking place; complaining rises to an all-time high. Some of you are saying, 'That's why I'm in transition, because somebody I'm hanging with is just complaining too much.' Whatever the case, complaining takes place.

In Exodus 16, we will discover three reasons the Israelites complained. We will also discover one way in which God responded to their complaining. We've already walked through chapter 15, and we recognized in verse 22, that the children of Israel were on the move. They had already crossed the Red Sea having been delivered out of Egypt from Pharaoh's hands. They had to make several stops along the way, and our passage describes their third stop after they crossed the Red Sea on their journey to the Promised Land. God has a place for His people. He has a designed destiny for His people, but on the way to the Promised Land there are things they must go through. There are some stops they must make. From the time they left Egypt until they entered the Promised Land, they made fifty stops. That's a lot of stops, and most of those stops were unnecessary. As a matter of fact, they stopped forty years longer than they should have. God only wanted them to go about eleven days, maybe a little bit longer than that, but they ended up taking forty years making stops and going in circles, in the same mess over and over, because they refused to listen, obey, and trust the Lord God Almighty.

So here we see they are on their third stop. They came across the Red Sea, then they were in the desert of Shur, next they were at Marah, now they are at Elim, and they are getting ready to move again. These moves are ordained by God. God was forcing them or challenging them to make these moves because these moves advanced them to where they are going. There are moves that are necessary moves for the transition process. As we look at the forty years, we see there were moves and stops that were unnecessary because they did not want to listen when God said listen.

In our reading, we'll look at God-ordained moves. That means that before they came across the Red Sea, before they departed Egypt, God had already ordained for them to make these moves. It was already in the script. God says in the book of Jeremiah, *"Before I formed you in your mother's womb I already knew you."* God says, 'I am not making up this map as you are en route to your destiny. I am not making up the map as you move along. I've already designed where you need to go, when you need to move, how quickly you need to move, and what takes place on the journey, because I want you to be ready by the time you arrive. So, none of this is a surprise to God.' Now the Israelites need to make sure that they are listening and trusting God.

Let's look at verse 1 of chapter 16: *"Then the whole community [The entire congregation] of Israel set out from Elim and journeyed into the wilderness of Sin, between Elim and Mount Sinai; they arrived there on the fifteenth day of the second month, one month after leaving the land of Egypt."*

It did not say one month after leaving the Red Sea. It said one month after leaving the land of Egypt. We do not know exactly how long they stayed when they moved to the oasis in the land of Elim. We do know they stayed several weeks. This is the longest stay they have had in one place so far on their journey. They went through the Red Sea to their first stop right there at Marah. It took them three days to get there and they stayed there one day, then they moved to their second stop at Elim where they stayed for a while.

In verse 2, we read: *"Then there too, the whole community complained about Moses and Aaron."* According to the scriptures, complaining is taking place. From this, recognize that we need to expect complaining when we are in transition. It's not that we want complaining; we should expect it, as it comes with the territory. You have to understand that there are a whole lot of different people here in this community. There are different personalities, different people, and different mindsets. You know when you have about a million people and you have about two million opinions. Everybody has their own idea on how things should be going. Samuel Chand, the great leader and disciple maker, said, "The difference between a person who leads a small company or a small church and the person who leads a large company or a large church is their capacity to handle pain." What he's saying is, the more responsibility you have, the more pain you have; the less responsibility you have, the less pain you have. The difference between somebody dealing with a small situation and someone dealing with a large situation is: can they handle the pain it takes to grow to the next level?

Here's what Chand says about church: "For every church there's one devil for every ten people; there's devils for every hundred people." He says, "The more people you have the more devils you have." Some people say they want a large church; how many devils do you want? If you have a hundred people, how many devils do you have? If you have five people, how many devils do you have?

What he's saying is, wherever there is progress, always

expect negativity to take a ride too. It just goes with it. It happens on your job. Do you know any negative people on your job? Do you know some complaining people on your job? You really can't say because you might be the one.

We see three reasons the Israelites complained:

1. Because of What They Missed

Verses 2-3 is telling us: *"There too the whole community of Israel complained about Moses and Aaron. If only the Lord had killed us back in Egypt."* These people are on another level. God has delivered them from Egyptian bondage, from slavery, and now they are missing where they came from. Understand this is their third move. They had to move from the Red Sea to Marah and then to Elim, which was a nice spot. It had twelve wells with sweet water and seventy palm trees. They were just relaxing and having a good time eating, flourishing, doing what God called them to do at that point. It was a layover, a temporary stop. They were never meant to stay there. God just let them stay there a little longer than they anticipated and they accustom to it, and now they are complaining when God has moved them again because of what they missed.

What did they miss? They missed three things about Egypt:

a) They missed Rations. They missed food. Verse 3 tells us: *"If only the Lord had killed us back in Egypt they moaned. [they murmured]; there we sat around pots filled with meat and ate all the bread we wanted."* Here's what they are missing: They are slaves; they are not eating steaks and filet mignon. They're eating scraps, leftovers, leeks and onions. They are getting whatever was left from the big house. God has delivered them from that type of lifestyle, that type of diet, that situation and they are now free, but they are missing what they used to eat when they were slaves. They are missing leftovers. They are complaining about being free and dreaming about what they used to have.

b) They are missing Routine. They have been slaves for four hundred years. Even though it was slavery, it was still what they were used to because they knew what to expect every day. What was their routine when they were slaves? Mostly just wake up in the morning and go to work; and when you go to work you slave all day. You work extra hard. Then after working extra hard all day, you come home, you eat, and you go to sleep. After going to sleep, you know what happens: you get up the next day and the cycle begins again. You do the same thing but on a different day. They're free now. They do not have to do that anymore. Now they are complaining because they miss their rations and also because they miss their routine. Even though it was monotonous, even though they were not receiving any payment, even though it was not beneficial to them in any way, it was still what they were used to. They knew what to expect. They missed the routines that they went through in slavery.

c) They missed their Reality. Everybody who was in this group was born in slavery. None of them knew what it meant to be free. None of them knew what it meant to have their own stuff and to be their own person. They had a slavery reality. It was a binding reality. It was a restricted reality. Whatever the situation, it was their reality. It was what they grew up in. It was all they knew. They saw their mother slaving. They saw their father slaving. They saw their cousin slaving. They saw their friends slaving. As a matter of fact, they had not been exposed to anything else but slavery. They missed it because now they have to function and learn a new reality now that they are free. How in the world are they missing bondage now that they are free? Because they missed their rations, they missed their routine, and they also missed their reality. It was a comfort zone for them.

Even though they despised it, they needed it as it gave them their identity. It made life simple. It made things predictable and left them thinking they could control it even though it was controlling them.

In verse 3, they say, *"If only the Lord had killed us back in Egypt."* 'We just wished the Lord had killed us before we became free because I'm do not like this free thing. We're not feeling this freedom thing. I'm supposed to be happy. We're supposed to be joyous, but right now we're mad. Let me tell you who we are mad at.' Verse 2 says, *"There, too, the whole community [not one or two] of Israel complained"* about the people who led them out. They complained about the leadership—the ones who help set them free—Moses and Aaron. They are putting all their frustrations on the people who came to help them.

The second reason they complained is because…

2. Their Feelings Created Imaginary Motives

Their feelings started creating imaginary motives in their minds. Motives of who? Moses and Aaron. They are saying, 'Your motives aren't even right.' They have followed Moses and Aaron all the way from Egypt across the Red Sea, but now they have concocted in their minds that Moses and Aaron did it for the wrong reasons. They thought Moses and Aaron did three things.

a) Deceived them. They thought Moses and Aaron tricked them to get out of Egypt. Verse 3: *"If only the Lord had killed us back in Egypt they moaned; there we sat around pots filled with meat and ate all the bread we wanted. But now, you have brought us into the wilderness to starve us all to death."* 'You deceived us. You told us you were going to get us out and we were going to go to the Promised Land. We don't see any land and we don't believe your promise. We're right here; we are not there. You have tricked us. You came down here and talked with all these big words—talking about God spoke with you on top of a mountain, and how a bush was burning, but it didn't burn up, and you took your shoes off—we should have known something wasn't right then. You're eighty years old. You must have Alzheimer's. You just tricked us. As a matter of fact, we know your history. We know that you killed a man when you were forty years old and you took off running. We did a background check on you. We recognize you. You are no good. We figured you out, man. Look at you and your brother, Aaron.' They thought Moses and Aaron had tricked them,

They also thought they:

b) Displaced them. Verse 3 says, *"There we sat around pots filled with meat and ate all the bread we wanted. But now, you have brought us into the wilderness to starve us all to death."* 'You stood before us and talked us up out of Egypt just to bring us to a place where we have to now depend on you. Now we are vulnerable. You're ego-tripping. You brought us brought us out of here. We can't go back to Pharaoh so what are we going to do now? We have to depend on you. We haven't received anything listening to your old crazy self. Your motives are not right.' The Israelites thought Moses and Aaron had deceived them, displaced them, and now…

They thought they:

c) Desired to destroy them. 'We know what you really want to do with us. You want to kill us.' Verse 3 goes on to say, *"But now, you have brought us into the wilderness to starve us all to death."* Why in the world would Moses go down to Egypt and do all this? Here's what I am trying to tell you: Do you know why the Israelites are having these creative thoughts in their minds? Because just like you and me, some of us can think ourselves into some bad stuff. Somebody who sits next to you in church has created in their mind what you are all about even without saying anything to you. Somebody on your job thinks you make more money than they do because you dress nice. They don't know that you know how to make Wal-Mart look like Neiman Marcus on you. They know how to design your life, and they design the reason you need to work in that position thinking you're trying to get their spot.

Whenever you start getting into your feelings, you start creating stuff that is not really true. Your situation is uncomfortable, and now, because you can't control it, you begin to think you need to do something that makes you feel better and you end up tearing down someone rather than building someone up. When you are uncomfortable, you say, 'I'm not going to be uncomfortable by myself.' You've heard the old adage: Misery loves company. That's all the children of Israel were doing right now. Their feelings are now creating imaginary motives. They tell Moses, 'You don't really want to help us. You're trying to destroy us. You're playing games.'

There is also another reason why the Israelites complained:

3. They Were Just Plain Moody

Look at verse 3 again: *"If only the Lord had killed us back in Egypt they moaned, there we sat around pots filled with meat and ate all the bread we wanted, but now you have brought us into this wilderness to starve us all to death."* Wait a minute! How are you going to skip over the place you just left, where you had an abundance of water and shade trees and you stayed there for several weeks? How are you going to skip over Marah where you had bitter water and God ended up performing a miracle there? How are you going to skip over what God did when you crossed the Red Sea and go all the way back to Egypt talking about how you should have died there? These Israelites have spiritual amnesia. The blessings of the Lord, in their minds, only last for so long because God can only be so good for so long. They are just moody.

Let me show you how moody they are: First of all, when they were in bondage for four hundred years they complained about their bondage.

They said, 'God, get us out of here.'

God says, 'Alright, I hear your cries. I'm going to send Moses to come get you out.' Moses comes down and Moses says, 'I don't want to go down there. I do not want to go. Moses, go down there.'

Moses says, 'Well, what am I going to tell them?'

God says, 'Just tell them that I sent you.'

Moses says, 'I can't go. As a matter of fact, I… I… I have a stuttering problem. I… I… I can't even tell Pharaoh to let my people go.' Whenever you don't want to do what God says to do you start creating stuff.

God says, 'You don't need to worry about that. Who do you think makes mouths anyway? If you don't want to talk right, don't worry about it. I'm going to send your brother, Aaron, to roll with you. Now, what's your excuse?'

Moses goes down there. He ends up telling the people, 'Let's go. Let's go! Let's get ready to roll up out of here.'

They became very excited. They rolled on out of Egypt and they arrived at the banks of the Red Sea. Remember what was happening: they were shouting, they were excited, they were dancing. They had an abundance of gold and silver. They had more stuff now than they ever had in their life, but they come to the Red Sea and what happens? They start talking about Moses and Aaron. 'Why did you bring us out here? We brought all this stuff. You brought us out here to die.'

Moses gets frustrated and says, 'Lord, what am I to do with these people?'

God says, 'Quit looking at Me, Moses. Stretch out your rod.'

What happens next? The sea opened up. They ran across. Now they are on the other side. God drowns Pharaoh's army in the Red Sea. Then what happens after that? They are excited again.

They have stopped complaining for now. Verses 1-21 of chapter 15 tells us they are so excited they wrote 21 verses about it. They put it in a song. "God delivered us." They are dancing. They are excited. Then God says, 'You all are going to have to get up out of here. You are going to have to leave the Red Sea and go to Marah.'

After they arrived in Marah, they become bitter because the water is bitter. They start complaining again until God works a miracle and makes the water sweet. They tasted the water and became happy again. Then they leave Marah and come to Elim. Now they are excited until God says it's time to leave Elim. What are they doing now? They're mad again. Moody.

Moses says, 'God, I do not know what I am going to get each day I wake up. I know you called me to lead them, but this is confusing.'

Why are they like this? Because they are led by their

feelings and not by their faith. They are like a child who always has to have one more thing to keep their attention. If you don't show them anything for too long, if they can't see any progress for too long, they'll start crying.

Finally, God has mercy on them and performs a miracle.

I know if you were God, some of you would be thinking: 'If these people, after all I have done for them, are complaining about what they are missing, have these imaginary motives that they have created in their minds, are complaining about everything, are happy one moment, and mad the next, I am not going to respond in a nice way. These people are ungrateful.' Oh, thank God, we are not God. Aren't you glad that you are not God? Because if you were God something a little different would happen. Right?

Let's start here in verse 4: *"But the Lord says to Moses, I'm going to rain down food from Heaven for you. Each day the people are going to go out and pick up as much food as they need for that day. I will test them on this to see whether or not they will follow my instructions."* Here's how God responds: He provided what they needed day by day. He says, 'I'm going to do this not because you deserve this. I'm going to provide you with food not one day, but everyday. You have to come and get it. I'm not going to do everything for you, but, in my mercy, I'm going to provide that.'

Here's what else God is going to do: He's going to prove who they are really upset with. Look at verses 7-8: Moses says, *"In the morning you will see the glory of the Lord because He has heard your complaints, which are against Him, not against us.*

Then Moses added, the Lord God, will give you meat to eat, and bread to satisfy you in the morning for He has heard all your complaints. What have we done? Yes, your complaints are against the Lord, not against us."

Moses said, 'You all have this thing twisted. You're frustrated with us because you're not making progress like you think we ought to be making progress. You're frustrated with us because we're not moving as fast as you think you need to move. Now you're taking it out on us when we're only following Him, but because you can't hear Him, you're going to be mad at us.' He says, 'You know what? We'll take it, but let me tell you who you are really mad at. You're really mad at God, which really means you're really mad at yourself because God is never wrong. So, the person you need to be mad at because things are not moving like you want it to move is yourself.'

Finally, God is going to position them to praise. Verse 7 says, *"In the morning you will see the glory of the Lord."* In their disobedience, God is still going to show His glory. That is still not the shouting part; here's the shouting part: *"Because He has heard your complaints which are against Him not us."* Everybody says, 'Lord, show me Your glory.' Are you sure you want to see His glory? See, His glory does not come just because you did good. His glory sometimes comes because you've been complaining too much. The presence of God does not just show up because you're right; He'll show up because you've been complaining too much. Well, what's the shouting point? Because no matter why He showed up, He showed up, and the people did not die. That ought to be a reason to praise.

Many want to hear a word from God. Conviction is a word from God. God says, 'I'm showing up because you have been complaining about everybody I've placed in your life to help you. You have not recognized it, but I didn't send anything that was going to be comfortable; I sent sandpaper. They're complaining about the help God sent to them.'

You can't stand your boss? That's why God sent you to that job, because if you're ever going to be a good supervisor, you have to report to one who is challenging and you must keep your composure. You complain about the help? You don't like them? Well, that's your help. Usually, God sends to us what's uncomfortable.

When you're in transition, don't complain about what you missed in Egypt. I don't know what your Egypt is. Your Egypt might have been your job. Your Egypt might have been your last relationship. What God is saying is this: Why are you complaining about what I delivered you from? Some might say, 'Even though they were bad... Even though she was challenging... Even though he was mean... it was a routine. I at least knew the challenge I had to deal with. At least when they disrespected me, I knew how they were going to reprimanded me and I knew when to expect it.'

Why are you missing it? I know why. For some people, it's not because the jobs aren't available. Some people can't get off food stamps, can't get off the government system and can't get off of Pharaoh's provisions. Here's why: it's not because jobs are not available—some people still have challenges because of their lifestyle, but that's not the majority of the people we are talking about. Most people are trying to manipulate the system because all they know is slavery. Their mother was on food stamps; their father was on food stamps; their grandma was on food stamps. Everybody worked the system and you ended up learning how to work—an Egyptian system—and you can't make it to the Promised Land with that mindset. You're fighting to stay in affordable housing. How many times are you going to hide the people who moved in with you knowing you're in violation in your Egypt?

What God is saying is this: 'Why are you missing those rations? Why are you complaining about your freedom.' You can get free, but can you manage your freedom? Do you know how to manage your deliverance? Or will you just complain about how much you miss your Egypt?

You'll be like this man who went to prison whose last name was Church. He went to prison for murder. He received a fifteen-year sentence, but for some reason he was released early. He was excited. His fellow inmates who were in prison told him, 'It's a whole new world out there.' He thought they were just jealous of him; but they were trying to prepare him. He was released from prison and was out ninety-six days. He ended up staying with a relative of a friend who was in prison. They gave him a decent place to live. When he went into prison, they weren't using cell phones, but when he was released, it was a whole new world. He felt alienated. Everything made him feel he could not handle the 'new' world as things had changed so much. He had been in bondage for so long, that once he was free again, the world was a different place.

He started trying to make his way through it, but he could not make the adjustment because he felt inadequate in this new season of his life. Here is what took place: He started trying to figure out ways to go back to prison. He started missing his job as a janitor in one of the prisons he was in. He burned down the house he was staying in and the cops still did not take him to jail. He said, 'Man, I can't even go back to jail right.' He then went down to the local place to eat. He ordered a lot of food, and ate all he could eat. He didn't have but thirty-one cents in his pocket. He told the manager, 'You go ahead and call the cops.' The manager told him, 'If you just leave I won't call the cops.' He said, 'I can't even go to jail right.' God is trying to keep him free, and, instead, he is running back to what God was trying to deliver him from. One day he received his wish and the cops came, arrested him and sent him to jail.

God said, 'I delivered you, but you can't be like a dog that returns to its vomit.' A dog is being purged by what made it sick. God delivers that dog and that dog ends up getting it all out and the dog looks at it, smells it, sees how it made him feel, and walks away. Because of the 'dog' in him, he goes back to where he was delivered from and licks it right back up and gets sick again because that's what he is used to.

Can you handle your deliverance when you get what you asked God for? Don't make up imaginary motives. Stop being mad at the people you like. Quit making up stuff about people because you are not happy. God is not really concerned about you being happy; He is concerned about your holiness. And sometimes He'll make you mad just to make you straight. Don't get caught up in your own mood swings. Let people know what they are going to get from you, and quit making the excuse: 'that's just how I am.' If that's how you are, you need to change.

Finally, expect God to perform a miracle of mercy. Expect to see God's glory. Expect God to open up some doors. Expect God to be merciful, but don't take His mercy for granted. Don't expect God to just keep doing and you keep complaining.

Jesus lived, died, and He did not complain, and He rose from the dead with more power. If you can hang on your cross through the pain without complaining, you, too, can rise with more power.

> "Then the whole community of Israel set out from Elim and journeyed into the wilderness of Sin, between Elim and Mount Sinai. They arrived there on the fifteenth day of the second month, one month after leaving the land of Egypt. There, too, the whole community of Israel complained about Moses and Aaron.
>
> "If only the Lord had killed us back in Egypt," they moaned. "There we sat around pots filled with meat and ate all the bread we wanted. But now you have

brought us into this wilderness to starve us all to death."

Then the Lord said to Moses, "Look, I'm going to rain down food from heaven for you. Each day the people can go out and pick up as much food as they need for that day. I will test them in this to see whether or not they will follow my instructions. On the sixth day they will gather food, and when they prepare it, there will be twice as much as usual."

So Moses and Aaron said to all the people of Israel, "By evening you will realize it was the Lord who brought you out of the land of Egypt. In the morning you will see the glory of the Lord, because he has heard your complaints, which are against him, not against us. What have we done that you should complain about us?" Then Moses added, "The Lord will give you meat to eat in the evening and bread to satisfy you in the morning, for he has heard all your complaints against him. What have we done? Yes, your complaints are against the Lord, not against us."

Exodus 16:1-8 (NLT)

6

Expect Confirmation When You're in Transition

If you pray as you read this chapter, I promise you that God will speak to you because whatever it is that you need you can always find in the Word of God. The Holy Spirit can take what you're reading and confirm it in you. God is that good. So expect confirmation as we continue studying the transitional period in the life of the Israelites.

If we're going to get to that place God has designed and destined for us, then we must go through transitions in many areas of our lives, but we don't want to just go through transitions; we want to *grow* through transitions. Are you going through some transition in your life right now? You know that God is moving you; God is changing something; God is doing something different in you. If you are in the same place spiritually this year as you were last year, something is wrong. If you open up yourself to what God wants to do in your life as you read this chapter, I promise that by the time you get to the end, God is going to speed up your transition process. He can make up time you thought you lost.

There are five things we've discovered so far that we should expect when in transition.

1) There will be **changes**.
2) There will be **challenges**.
3) There will be a **character check**.
4) There will be **code compliance**, and unfortunately,
5) There will be some **complaining**.

God has already factored complaining into your journey. It's not that He wants us to complain; He just expects it. It's not that you should want to complain; but it is expected every now and then. Frustration will set in during a time of transition. Wouldn't you much rather know ahead of time where God wants you to be. Of course, but that is not always the case.

As we continue in our journey with the Israelites, we find that, during transition, we need to expect confirmation. To confirm means to establish the truth. The truth will be established by pieces of evidence. God tells the Israelites, 'If you want to know the truth about this journey that you're on, I'm going to give you pieces of evidence that it was not the pizza you ate last night that made you have some dreams. It's not just something you went through. It's not just some cruel experience. I'm going to give you pieces of evidence that the truth is, when you left Egypt, you heard My word, and even where you are right now, after those transitions you went through, guess what? You are on the right track. You're on the right road.'

As we look at this, we'll understand how the Israelites received confirmation from God. They were in the right place at the right time and were ready to move in the right direction. The children of Israel had been delivered from four hundred years of Egyptian bondage under the hand of Pharaoh. God brought them across the Red Sea, drowned Pharaoh's army, and now has a Promised Land waiting for the children of Israel. All they have to do is go on an eleven-day journey, maybe thirteen days, to get there. However, it ends up taking them forty years with them having to make fifty stops. Several of those stops were unnecessary. They could have arrived to the place where God was taking them a lot quicker if they had simply obeyed Him.

All five previous chapters have discussed necessary stops. In this chapter, we'll present another necessary stop. They have already come across the Red Sea, they moved from the Red Sea to Marah, then they moved on to Elim, and now they are in the wilderness of Sin. They are in a situation where they need to know if this is where God wants them to be? The Israelites are saying, 'It's frustrating. We can't see anything. We can't see what's going on. It's been a treacherous journey for us.' The complaints are just going and going. God hears their complaints. Then God says, 'I recognize where My people are. They need confirmation. They need to hear from Me.'

This isn't the first time God gives confirmation to His people. Not just one confirmation; He's given them several confirmations throughout this process. Throughout this whole journey, He's been giving confirmation after confirmation after confirmation. Do you know that God is so patient with us that He knows how to confirm for us when we need it? There are five things that the Israelites went through so they could receive confirmation and clarity that God was with them.

The first thing is...

1. They Heard a Proclamation

Verse 9 says, *"Then Moses said to Aaron, announce this to the entire community of Israel: present yourselves before the Lord for He has heard your complaints."* God is saying, 'Alright, Moses, I've heard My children crying. They are complaining and I have heard it.' As we've seen before, God responded to the Israelites with mercy. Here's how God responded with mercy in their complaining: They had been in Egyptian slavery for four hundred years. They had only been free for a little over a month. They had been conditioned for over four hundred years, tied up in a situation with a certain lifestyle and a certain way of living and a different mentality. They have only been free and have had to learn a whole new way of living in just a little over a month. God responds with mercy because He knew where His people were. God had a bigger picture. He understood they were not going to get over four hundred years of thinking in a month.

If you have been living a certain way for a long time, it's going to take time for you to be weaned off of your old mindset. Yes, God could come in and touch you. Guess what? There are some things that you will need to re-learn. There are some things we need to teach in our deliverance services. You can be delivered, but can you manage your deliverance? You have to walk through it as deliverance is a process. God says, 'I'm going to respond with mercy'; but Moses is frustrated. In fact, Moses became upset several times. He was upset when they were complaining at the Red Sea. He was upset when they were complaining at Marah. Moses, right now, is frustrated, but God had already put a plan in place for Moses.

Let's review verse 9: *"Then Moses said to Aaron, announce this to the entire community."* God had already given Moses someone throughout his entire life so that when Moses was frustrated, that person could speak to the people on his behalf. This is why it is very important to understand what you're good at and what you're not good at. This is why it is important for you to know when you need to talk and when you need to send someone to talk for you. Moses, right now, is hotter than fish grease. God says, 'I already have a plan in place for, Moses. I've put someone in your life who can help you when you have a tough time communicating things My way.' Some of you are thinking, 'Don't judge Moses. He did not want to talk in the first place. He did not want to go down to Egypt and tell Pharaoh to let My people go. He started acting like he had a stuttering problem.' God said, 'Don't worry about it. I already have someone going with you. I'll send over to you your brother. He's going to be your mouthpiece. He's going to be the one who speaks to the people and to Pharaoh on My behalf, so don't worry about it. I've assigned someone for this season in your life.'

We have to recognize how to properly use the people God has already placed in our lives, because we have to make sure that we do not end up doing what God has assigned someone else to do for us. Moses is the prophet; Aaron is the priest. Moses is a little rough around the edges. The reason Moses had to run and leave Egypt the first time is because he killed someone. Moses had a record. He was a murderer. Moses had an attitude. The role of a prophet is to speak to the people on behalf of God. If you look at the Old Testament prophets, you'll see that they didn't seem very nice. They would come straight at you. They were direct. They would get up in your face and say, 'Now that's what the Lord said.' They would cut you up, leave you bleeding, and then say, 'You have to do what God has told me to tell you to do because that's how it is.'

Now the job of the priest was to speak to God on behalf of the people. The priest was a bit more sensitive. He was a bit more patient. Moses, being a prophet, recognized right now might not be a good time for him to talk with the people because he would tell them what the Lord says, and it might hurt their feelings, so Aaron, had to go and make the announcement.

Right now, is the time for the priest. Aaron is told to make the announcement.' That's what a proclamation is. And if they are going to get the confirmation that they need from

God, here's the first thing that they need: a proclamation. What was the first proclamation?

a) Draw closer to God. Verse 9 says, *"Moses said to Aaron, announce this to the entire community of Israel, present yourselves before the Lord."* He's saying, 'God has heard your complaining.' Notice that God does not push them away. He says, 'Come closer. I know you're complaining because you don't understand some things, so come closer. Draw nearer to Me.' Notice what Aaron says: *"Present yourselves."* God is saying, 'I'm not going to force you into My presence. You have to make a decision on your own to individually come closer to Me.'

b) You have His attention. Verse 9 says, *"Present yourselves before the Lord for He has heard your complaining."* After hearing their complaining, God told Moses to tell them, to draw closer to Him. That's not how He wants them to get His attention, but they received it. Their complaining has God's ears tuned in to their station.

First they heard a proclamation. Next...

2. They Saw a Manifestation

Look at verse 10: *"And as Aaron spoke, to the whole community of Israel, they looked out toward the wilderness; there they could see the awesome glory of the Lord in the cloud."* They heard a proclamation, but now they saw a manifestation. How did they see a manifestation of God?

a) They were placed in the Proper Position. They could not stay where they were. What was their proper position? *"They looked out toward the wilderness."* Apparently, if they looked out toward the wilderness, that's not where they were looking before God told them to draw closer. They looked in another direction. They were placed in the proper position.

In other words, they were not going to see a manifestation of God in the position they were in previously, so they had to look toward the wilderness. Here's what happened when they were placed in the proper position:

b) They saw God's Powerful Presence. As they turned toward the wilderness, *"they could see the awesome glory of the Lord in the cloud."* They could see the visible glory of God. They can't see God; they see God's glory. God manifested Himself in a cloud.

Now understand this: they are looking toward the wilderness. We don't know which wilderness we are talking about here. We just know they are in the wilderness of Sin. To get to the Promised Land, they have to go through the wilderness of Sinai. Sin is here; Sinai is there. It may be that God ended up manifesting Himself over in the wilderness of Sinai to show them, right now, don't worry about anything because My glory is going where you are about to go, and I'll be waiting on you when you get there. I'm the same God here that I'll be over there.

If He was talking about the wilderness of Sin, He says, I want you to know I am around you right now. I hear your complaining, but let Me show you My glory. I'm here with you. They heard a proclamation. They heard a manifestation. Third . . .

3. God Raised Their Expectations

Whenever you see someone coming out of a place where they have been for four hundred years (or for any long period of time) as is the case of the Israelites, even though they are free, they are insecure. You can cry to get out of a situation, but can you handle it once you get out? You can cry to get out of a marriage, but can you handle your singleness and the loneliness that comes with it? You have to be able to walk through what you have been delivered out of if you are going to survive. Be careful what you ask to get out of, because what you get out of might kill you.

Whenever insecurity is at its highest, expectations are at their lowest. You're not expecting God to do a lot; you're not expecting people to do too much. Your faith in God, your faith in people, your faith in other things is at its lowest, and God recognizes that and He says, 'You know what? They don't really believe in much right now. They have gone through so much in this last month and a half that they may feel where I'm taking them, I'm taking them too fast. Don't worry about it. I am trying to get them to their destination fast, so I have to have a speedy delivery. I have somewhere for them to go, so they just need to go on ahead and travel at the speed at which I am going. I am not going to slow it down for them, so I have to raise their expectations in the middle of it all, because we have a long way to go.'

How did God raise the expectations of the Israelites? In verse 12, God says to Moses: *'I have heard the Israelites' complaints, now tell them in the evening you will have meat to eat, and in the morning, you will have all the bread you want."* They were crying because they did not have anything to eat. In verse 13 we read, *"That evening vast numbers of quail flew in and covered the camp; and the next morning, the area around the camp was wet with dew."*

God raised their expectations. They were crying to Moses and Aaron because they had plenty of meat to eat when they were with Pharaoh. They are exaggerating because it wasn't good meat. It was leftovers; it wasn't the best stuff. They are crying about how they miss their Egyptian slave food. God hears their complaints and He says, 'I knew you would be hungry at this point in the journey. Nothing catches Me by surprise. You must understand that I have to wean you off of what you had, and I am going to have to change your taste buds. I have to change what you crave. So it's going to take a while for you to do without in the transition, because I'm taking away from you what you're used to having and not giving you everything consistently right now. I have to change what your taste buds go after. Your taste is bad; you're still chasing after the wrong people and they have a million dollar body and a ten cents soul. You've been craving the wrong thing.'

How is God raising their expectations? God says...

a) They will have emergency assistance. What is the emergency assistance? Verse 12 says: *"I have heard the Israelites' complaints, now tell them in the evening..."* Apparently, this is not the evening. This is earlier in the day. God says, 'I am about to hook you up, not tomorrow, but I am going to rush order something for you this evening. I am faster than

UPS or Federal Express.' The Israelites will have emergency assistance. The Bible reads, *"Tell them in the evening, you will have meat to eat… That evening vast numbers of quail flew in and covered the camp."*

God said, 'I'm not just going to send it your way, I'm going to have you covered. I'm not going to give you left-overs. I'm going to fly in something fresh.' This is not the first time God made birds come in to take care of the people. Later on, He did it again. Allow me to show you how it happened the second time.

The second time, the Bible says that birds flew in one direction and God sent a wind to make them change direction to come in the direction of His people. When they came in the direction of His people, they didn't fly by the people; they landed where His people were, because God spoke to the birds and said, 'You all will end up being used because My people need assistance.' He says, 'I'm going to fly in what you need. I'm redirecting and changing the winds so that what was going to fly past you is going to fly in your direction because you need something now.'

The people had emergency assistance.

b) They will have long term provision. God says, 'It's good for Me to meet your need today; but I do not want to just meet your need today. Today, I just want to get you stabilized, but you know you are going to have to eat after today.' God is saying, 'I'm not just going to give you emergency assistance; I'm going to give you a long-term process—a plan.' How is He going to do that? Let's look back at verse 12: *"The Lord said to Moses, I have heard the Israelites'* *complaints, now tell them in the evening you will have meat to eat, and in the morning, you will have all the bread you want."* Let's see if that happened. Verse 13 says, *"That evening vast numbers of quail flew in and covered the camp; and the next morning, the area around the camp was wet with dew. When the dew evaporated a flaky substance as fine as frost blanketed the ground."*

The first thing that came in covered the ground. The second thing that came in the very next morning also covered the ground. God is telling the children of Israel, 'No matter how you look at it, no matter how you call on Me, I have you covered. You are covered for the short term and you will be covered for the long term.' What they were going to eat for the next forty years had just shown up on the ground.

They heard a proclamation. They saw a manifestation. God raised their expectations. Fourth...

4. They Needed Some Clarification

Why did they need some clarification? There was something in this whole process that was not clear to them. Look at verse 15: *"The Israelites were puzzled when they saw it. What is it? They asked each other. They had no idea what it was."* God has manifested Himself. God has sent them something in the morning and they do not even know what it is. They looked at it and they did not even recognize their blessing. They needed some clarification because...

a) They only saw something Flaky. They heard what Moses said. They heard Aaron the things had spoken to them. They all heard what the both stated to the masses.

They had just finished eating real good last night on some quail—real meat—but now it's morning time. They wake up and they see something frosty and flaky on the ground, but it is not the cereal Tony the Tiger endorses. Something is 'flaky' about this situation. God said He was going to send all the bread they needed, but all they have right now is something that's flaky. They saw something flaky, but...

b) Moses saw God's Favor. How did Moses see God's favor? Look at verse 15: *"...and Moses told them, it is the food the Lord has given you to eat."* Moses received a revelation because He had godly conversation. You cannot get spiritual revelation talking to people with carnal conversation. Watch who you're talking to. The very thing they needed, the very thing God said He was about to do, they were about to miss it talking to each other. Moses then said, 'Let me show you my solution. I've already talked to God, and God has already told me what it is. Let me clarify: the very thing that you are judging incorrectly is the very thing God is using to provide provision for us the next forty years of our lives.'

Last, we understand...

5. They Received Their Confirmation

Verse 12 reads, *"The Lord said to Moses..I have heard the Israelites' complaints, now tell them in the evening you will have meat to eat, and in the morning, you will have all the bread you want. Then you will know that I am the Lord your God."* God's bestowing of meat and bread on the Israelites is their confirmation about Him. It was never about the food in the first place.

God says, 'What I am doing is: I'm introducing another side of Me that you may not even understand as of yet. I don't want you questioning, wondering, or guessing. I don't want you looking at Me asking, 'What is it?' I want you to know who I am.' Here are four things the Israelites could know in their confirmation about God:

a) God is present. How do I know He's present? Because He says *"I am."* What does "I am" mean? If you know anything about God's *am*-ness, God is saying, 'I want you to understand who I am today. I am the same God in the past as I am today. I am present. I am here right now.'

b) God is Powerful. He says, *"I am the Lord your God."* This means He is sovereign. The last part of this is 'reign,' and the only people who reign are kings. He is the Lord of all the universe. Not only is He present, but He is powerful. He is in control of everything. God says, 'If you can't understand that by how I made those birds fly into your camp, if you can't understand that by how I made honey buns appear on the ground for you, then something is wrong with you. I gave you dinner in the evening. You slept all night and you woke up to this. You have bread in the morning and you did not have to cook anything.' While they were sleeping, God was cooking. They did not have to do anything to receive all that food. God said, 'I am. I am powerful. I am the Lord.' Not just that, but ...

c) God is Personal. He says, "I am the Lord your God." He is a personal God. If I say, 'I am your God, that means I know your name, and since I know your name, I knew what you needed before you called My name. If I am your God and I am personal, what I have for you is tailor-made and nobody can get what I have for you.' He says, 'Israel, I am your God. That means, I am not everybody else's God. I am My own people's God. Since I am your God, that means you are My children, and I am not a "deadbeat dad" who is late on his payments. I always take care of my child support.' He is saying, 'I want to make sure you know that I am present, powerful, and personal.'

d) God keeps His Promises. God keeps His promises because He has shown Himself to be a provider. God says, 'Right now, everything you needed I've blessed you with and blessed you beyond what you were complaining about. You were complaining about food and I sent you quail. I sent you some fresh stuff. You were complaining about all the food and bread you did not have, and I ended up sending you bread—not just for one day, but for the rest of your time in the wilderness. Here's how I am going to do it: I am going to give you bread six days of the week, and on that sixth day, I am going to give you double, because on the seventh day, I do not want you to do anything. I want you to make that the Sabbath day.'

'I don't want you to forget that I am the Lord your God, and I want you all to still praise Me like I am still your God. I don't want you to complain, get the food, and get the blessing, and then forget about Me on the Sabbath day. So I am not sending any food on the Sabbath day. You're going to have to double up on everything on the sixth day. You're going to have to eat half of it on that day and then have the rest of it on the seventh day. On the seventh day, that is the day you better worship Me, because when I get through doing this, I don't want you to act like you forgot who I am. I want you to know that I am the Lord your God.'

You may think I am only talking about the Israelites, but do you need some confirmation from the Lord? Do you need to hear God speaking? Right now, you're saying, 'God, I need to know if I am on the right track. I need to know if You're still with me. I need to know if I am just crazy for having this dream, for starting this business, for going in this direction. When I started, I had peace, but as I traveled down the road, I faced some changes and challenges. I had to go through some stuff. You were checking my character, and right now, I need to know if You are still with me.'

Do you need some confirmation? The children of Israel heard a proclamation; that proclamation was simply, 'Draw closer to God.' In the book of James, the Bible says, "*Draw nigh to Me, and I'll draw nigh to you.*"

If you're going to get confirmation, the first thing you have to do is get closer to God. When you get closer to God there are certain things that cannot hang closer to you, because demons tremble at the name of Jesus. How do I get closer to God? How does God show up? God says He inhabits the praises of His people. Can you praise the Lord? You say, 'I need to know that God is speaking to me. I have some major decisions to make. I have some things I have been talking to God about. I need to know beyond the shadow of a doubt.' God says, 'The first thing you have to do is come a little closer to Me.' When praises go up God begins to come closer. He inhabits the praises of His people.

If you get in the presence of God, the devil cannot mess with you. The devil is a serpent; he is a snake. Let me tell you how you deal with real snakes on an airplane: You don't have to leave the cockpit. All you have to do is take the plane up to a higher altitude because snakes can't breathe at a high altitude. So, when you enter God's presence through praise, the devil can't hang with you, because you're getting closer to God.

You have to make sure that you raise your expectations. Just believe God. I may not be able to see it with my eyes, but I believe God! I've been praying too much, waiting too long, and crying too much to stop believing now. When I look back over my life, God has never let me down—not one time. That's why I needed some clarification. I needed to know it was the Lord who was about to do something great in my life. If you know who the Lord is, you'll recognize Him when He says, 'I am the Lord your God.' He says, 'I know what you want. I know what you need. Right now, you can't see it because I am about to fly it in.' Continue looking because your blessing is on the way. Expect it!

> Then Moses said to Aaron, "Announce this to the entire community of Israel: 'Present yourselves before the Lord, for he has heard your complaining.'" And as Aaron spoke to the whole community of Israel, they looked out toward the wilderness. There they could see the awesome glory of the Lord in the cloud.

Then the Lord said to Moses, "I have heard the Israelites' complaints. Now tell them, 'In the evening you will have meat to eat, and in the morning you will have all the bread you want. Then you will know that I am the Lord your God.'"

That evening vast numbers of quail flew in and covered the camp. And the next morning the area around the camp was wet with dew. When the dew evaporated, a flaky substance as fine as frost blanketed the ground. The Israelites were puzzled when they saw it. "What is it?" they asked each other. They had no idea what it was.

And Moses told them, "It is the food the Lord has given you to eat."

Exodus 16:9-15 (NLT)

Focus Verse: Verse 12: "Then you will know that I am the Lord your God."

7

Expect Conflict When You're in Transition

By following the journey of the Israelites, we have discovered that when a person or an organization is in transition, there are many things they must expect to encounter along the way. The six things that we have learned thus far that should not surprise us as are: *changes, challenges,* a *character check, code compliance, complaining,* and *confirmation.*

All this took place with the Israelites because there was conflict coming their way. As God enabled the Israelites to face conflict in transition, we will see that two things are necessary if we are going to face conflict and come out victorious. This is when we handle conflict God's way. Everything up until this point was internal. God had to take them through six different things because He was preparing them for a fight they never expected. God told them, 'I had to do all of that because there is something that you don't know about that is approaching you and I had to get you ready. So, even though I had to take you through six things, nothing was wasted. You were in boot camp and you did not even know it.' In boot camp, you lose some things you came into the camp with. Times get challenging, your money gets funny and your change can get strange during this season. You also have to develop and learn about your new relationships while at the same time let old ones go.

In verse 8, we recognize where they are: "*While the people of Israel were still at Rephidim, the warriors of Amalek attacked them.*" They had moved all the way from the wilderness of Sin and now they are at this place called Rephidim. Rephidim simply means resting place. After all they had gone through, they had now come to a place where they could exhale and rest. According to verses 1-7, they rested, but right where they were resting is where the enemy showed up.

In the Kingdom of God, there are no vacations. S atan does not take vacations. Christians don't take vacations. You cannot take a vacation from praying. The day you take a vacation from praying is the day you'll be in a bad place. You don't get to take a vacation because the day you take a vacation from praying and trusting God is the day you are setting yourself up for failure and attack. That is when the enemy comes—right when you are trying to rest. Verse 8 reads, "*While the people of Israel were still at Rephidim, the warriors of Amalek attacked them.*"

We understand that there is external conflict coming their way. Everything they had been dealing with up to this point had been among themselves. God had been allowing them to have conflict with one another and with their leadership, and He worked things out with them because He knew somebody who did not care anything about them was coming to destroy them. God says, 'I can deal with you while you're talking crazy. Moses can deal with you while you're talking crazy, and vice-versa, because we're family, but there is something on the outside that does not care about any of that. The Amalekites are coming.'

Israel, if you're going to deal with the Amalekites, here are three things you need to do:

1. You Need the Right Strategy

Looking at verse 9, we read: *"Moses commanded Joshua, Choose men to go out and fight the army of Amalek for us. Tomorrow, I will stand at the top of the hill holding the staff of God in my hand."* We see three things here when you need the right strategy:

a) You need a ground Attack. Ground attack means you get in front of it. Verse 9 says, *"Moses commanded Joshua, Choose men to go out and fight the army of Amalek for us."* That means they had to go down to where the enemy was. Amalek means valley dwellers. These are low living people. These are people who are on a lower level in their mindset, action, and everything they do. Right now, Israel is going to have to fight the enemy at a lower level. They have to face the Amalekites because the Amalekites are going to face them. Israelites, you do not get to run right now. You must go face them. Get in front of them.

b) You need an air Attack. Air attack means you get above it. Moses says, *"Tomorrow, I will stand at the top of the hill."* Here's what he is saying to Joshua: 'I want you to deal with it face to face on that level. As the leader, I have to deal with it on a different level. I have to look at this thing with a different strategy than the strategy you're using, because if I go higher I can see how we can really deal with it. While you're fighting down there, I'm going to deal with it from the top.'

c) You need the right kind of Weapons. What kind of weapons are you going to need for this? Moses says he will be "*holding the staff of God in my hand.*" We have two weapons: the staff and God. If you have the staff and you don't have God, you are still in trouble. If you have God, but did not pick up the staff He told you to pick up, you are still in trouble. God gave them the tools to fight this fight. He said, 'Don't look for Me to do for you what you can do for yourself. I gave you something to deal with this enemy before the enemy showed up. Moses, I gave you a staff before you even went in to deal with Pharaoh. You've been carrying this staff and it helped you cross the Red Sea. This staff has helped you in so many other ways, and now it is about to help you in battle. So don't worry about it. Before the conflict showed up I gave you the weapons to deal with it.'

2. You Need the Right Kind of Support

What kind of support do you need? Those who battle

on the field. Verse 9 reads, *"Moses commanded Joshua, Choose men to go out and fight the army of Amalek for us. Tomorrow, I will stand at the top of the hill holding the staff of God in my hand."*

For those who battle on the field, you can:

a) Tell them your Expectations. With the right kind of support, you'll have somebody who battles on the field who has the kind of trust-worthy character that you can tell them what you expect. Moses gave Joshua his expectations. He delegated the assignment of choosing the fighting men to him. Moses had his own assignment that he would carry out.

Those who battle on the field:

b) Do not hesitate with Execution. In verse 10, we see the execution: *"So Joshua did what Moses had commanded and fought the army of Amalek."* When you have people battling on the field, there is no arguing, there are no hindrances, and there is no back and forth. When you are in battle, you do not have time for issues. You need someone who can say, 'This is what we want done. Handle it.' 'This is what I need done. Can you do the job?' 'If you cannot do the job, Joshua, I will find somebody who can. Right now, there is an attack and when you're in war we don't have time for your feelings to get in the way because people will get hurt.'

Sometimes you have to fight with hurt feelings. Sometimes you have to go to work when you don't feel like it. You have to still raise those kids even though they get on your last nerves. It's not about your feelings. Like Mike Tyson said, "Everybody who gets in the ring to box has a strategy until they get hit." When you get hit, you realize that your strategy is not going to work right now. We just have to go for it.

Those who battle on the field:

c) Need the right kind of Support. Tell them your expectations, and if they don't hesitate with execution, then let them be. However, you don't just need those who battle on the field, you need those who battle on the hill.

There are three things about those who battle on the hill. Let's look at verse 10: *"So Joshua did what Moses had commanded and fought the army of Amalek. Meanwhile, Moses, Aaron, and Hur climbed to the top of a nearby hill."*

1) Those who battle on a hill are trusted with Elevation. Moses did not take everybody with him to the top. There is a certain mindset that those on the ground have to have. There is a certain mindset that those on the hill have to have. You can't have too many chiefs on the hill. You need all the Indians in the battlefield. You can trust certain people the higher you go. The higher you go up the less people can be close to you. Not everybody is being elevated for the right reason. With elevation comes trust.

2) Those who battle on the hill engage in Evaluation. Look again at verses 10-11: *"Meanwhile, Moses, Aaron, and Hur climbed to the top of a nearby hill. As long as Moses held up the staff in his hand the Israelites had the advantage, but whenever he dropped his hands, the Amalekites gained the advantage."* Moses' arms became so tired he could no longer hold them up. So, Aaron and Hur found a stone for him to sit on. They then stood on each side of Moses holding up his hands. They recognized that they are not on top of the hill with the leader just to tell everybody they were on top of the hill. They recognized they are on top of the hill because they are there to evaluate their leader and their situation by looking at the battle on the ground. They realize that as their leader goes, so goes the battle. Their job is to study how their leader is doing.

They notice that when Moses' hands are up they are winning. When their leader's hands are down they are losing. So, next they...

3) Carry out an assignment of Alleviation. Aaron and Hur's assignment is to alleviate the pressures of the leader. They recognized that their assignment was not to cause more problems for their leader. It was not to cause more drama for their leader. It was to make sure that their leader could be drama-free so he could do what he needed to do on the hill. In battle, you don't need more drama around you when you're trying to focus; you need somebody who's battling on the ground. The problem is, most people who are not fighting on the ground or on the hill are just sitting around waiting for somebody else to finish the job. How did Aaron and Hur alleviate the pressures of their leader?

Verse 12 says, *"So Aaron and Hur found a stone for him to sit on. Then they stood on each side of Moses holding up his hands."* They recognized that if they held up their hands, they were going to lose. They recognized who God had chosen and anointed for that season, and they said, 'Our job is not to hold up our hands, but to hold up your hands.' During this time, you have to have around you secure people who are strong enough, whose hands you do not have to hold through every little situation. They must have enough sense to say, 'Our leader needs us right now, so we have to hold up his hands because when his hands are stronger, everybody else is winning, but when we're not holding our leader's hands up, then, guess what? Everybody is losing.' That goes for your household. That goes for your job. That goes for your church. That goes for your friendships. There's somebody assigned in the group of people you are in whose hands need to be held up, and if you're not humble enough to see whose hands need to be held up, you will lose.

How can we minimize the stress on your life right now? The text says, *"They stood on each side of Moses holding up his hands. So his hands held steady until sunset."* They held up Moses' hands until they became tired, but they held them up nonetheless. They held them up the entire day. You have to have people around you who are not so focused on their own ministry, or on their own agenda. That is why you can't have just anyone holding up your hands because some people are only there to get a hand out. This season is for every hand to be on deck. When people are in your life and you have an assignment, you cannot have anybody who's distracted holding your hands, because when the battle is going on you'll need people who are focused.

You need the right strategy, you need the right kind of support, and third...

3. You Will Achieve the Right Kind of Success

If you did it God's way, you will get God's results. Sometimes that may look like a loss as it seemed when Jesus was on the cross, but we know that He won in the end. He said, *"Father, forgive them for they know not what they do."* He was saying, 'You are killing Me, but you don't recognize that you are helping Me, because if you don't kill Me, I will not fulfill My purpose. Go ahead, drive the nails in My hands. Even though I'm hurting now, catch Me in three days. You are going to see Me stronger, wiser, and bigger than I have ever been in My life, because I was born to suffer; but I was also born to reign.'

You will achieve the right kind of success. Verse 13 says, *"As a result Joshua overwhelmed Amalek."* The enemy did not have a chance when all of God's people were on the same page. It was an overwhelming victory.

The people did three things after the victory.

1) Write it Down. Verse 14 says, *"After the victory, the Lord instructed Moses, write this down on a scroll as a permanent reminder."* God says, 'I don't ever want you to forget what I just did in your life. As a matter of fact, I want you to put it on paper in case you have spiritual amnesia in the future. When you come across another enemy that looks strong, I want you to remember your first fight and how I helped you gain the victory. I want you to pull that paper out and say, 'God has helped me before.' I want you to pull it out and show your enemy and say, 'Bring it on if you want to. I have a victory under my belt." So, write it down.

2) Say it Loud. The text says, *"Write this down on a scroll as a permanent reminder, and read it aloud to Joshua."* Why read it aloud to Joshua? Because God had already spoken to Moses in some way about Joshua, so Moses knew there was something special about Joshua. Later on, we'll see that Joshua was the one who was going to take the children of Israel into the Promised Land. Moses had a spirit of deliverance. Joshua had a spirit of ushering in. You have to know what you have been called to do in each season of your life. If God has called you to deliver some people from some stuff, then that means you have to go through more hell than some people will have to go through. You have a deliverance ministry and that's why God keeps calling people to hang on to you so you can help deliver them from situations that they are in.

If you have Joshua's anointing, God will open doors for you to enter into new seasons when you make a move at the right time. Moses had to hit the water; Joshua just had to walk through. Do you recognize that God has a plan for your life? Whatever He's called you to do, realize that you have an anointing on your life to open doors and usher people in.

3) Worship. In verses 15-16, we read: *"Moses built an altar there and named it Yahweh-Nissi, which means The Lord is my banner. He said they have raised their fists against the Lord's throne. So now the Lord will be at war with Amalek generation after generation."* What God is saying is, 'Anybody who looks like Amalek, anybody who comes up against you as Amalek did,

I will be at war with them.' Moses is saying, 'After this victory, I have to worship, I have to build an altar, I have to give a sacrifice, I have to give some praise because what God has just said to me is simply this: 'Whenever they step up against you they've stepped up against Me.''

Some battles you do not have to fight; you just have to show up. And the Bible says in Romans 8:31 'If God [be] for us (you), He's more than the whole world against you.' Let me tell you what kind of victory you are going to have: You're going to have a hands-on victory. Joshua had his hands on the enemy; Aaron and Hur had their hands on the leader; Moses had his hands on the staff. Let me tell you who God had His hands on: He had His hands on everybody. He had His hands in the battle. You're about to have a hands-on victory, because when God has His hands on you no weapon formed against you shall be able to prosper.

> While the people of Israel were still at Rephidim, the warriors of Amalek attacked them. Moses commanded Joshua, "Choose some men to go out and fight the army of Amalek for us. Tomorrow, I will stand at the top of the hill, holding the staff of God in my hand."
>
> So Joshua did what Moses had commanded and fought the army of Amalek. Meanwhile, Moses, Aaron, and Hur climbed to the top of a nearby hill. As long as Moses held up the staff in his hand, the Israelites had the advantage. But whenever he dropped his

hand, the Amalekites gained the advantage. Moses' arms soon became so tired he could no longer hold them up. So Aaron and Hur found a stone for him to sit on. Then they stood on each side of Moses, holding up his hands. So his hands held steady until sunset. As a result, Joshua overwhelmed the army of Amalek in battle.

After the victory, the Lord instructed Moses, "Write this down on a scroll as a permanent reminder, and read it aloud to Joshua: I will erase the memory of Amalek from under heaven." Moses built an altar there and named it Yahweh-Nissi (which means "the Lord is my banner"). He said, "They have raised their fist against the Lord's throne, so now the Lord will be at war with Amalek generation after generation."

Exodus 17:8-16 (NLT)

Focus Verse: Verse 8: "While the people of Israel were still at Rephidim, the warriors of Amalek attacked them."

8

Expect Conjecture When You're in Transition

As we travel with the Israelites, thus far, we've observed seven things to expect as we go through transitions in our lives: changes, challenges, a character check, code compliance, complaining, confirmation, conflict, and now conjecture. They went through all these things before they entered the Promised Land. We can identify with the Israelites because we, too, go through these seven things as we go through transitions in our lives. We thank God that He did not respond with wrath or with anger. God said, I understand you have been in Egyptian bondage for four hundred years and you have only been free for a little over a month, so I know you have to make some major adjustments, therefore, I am going to respond with confirmation. I want to let them know they are in the right place at the right time following the right God on their way to the right destination. God encouraged them not to quit right now. He did not want them to get discouraged before they entered the Promised Land even though they ran into conflict as they did battle with the Amalekites over whom God gave them victory. The devil does not want you to reach your destination, even as he did not want the children of Israel to reach the destination God had for them.

You may have to deal with your internal stuff; but God is saying, I just want you to get your internal stuff right so that when something attacks you from the outside you won't be insecure. You'll know who you are. You'll know who to trust. You'll know who to deal with.

By looking at the Israelites' lives as they went through their period of transition, we notice that we need to expect conjecture. Conjecture is the formation or expression of an opinion without sufficient evidence or proof. To summarize it, it's a guess or speculation. It is a Latin word that comes from two words: *con* which means together, and *jecere* which means to throw. It indicates when somebody only has a piece of evidence or a piece of information. What they don't know, they end up making up the rest and coming up with their own conclusion. They just throw something together and call it the truth. Because they do not know the whole story, they create one.

Do you know of anyone whom you have never told any of your business to, yet they know more about your business and they end up telling others about your business which is nothing close to the truth? It's conjecture!

Conjecture is a lie. It is a million dollar word for a ten cents attitude. Conjecture is taking place in the scriptures. I withdrew four things from our scripture reading that I will share with you: two things about conjecture, one thing about how to deal with conjecture, and the fourth thing you'll see is the benefits of dealing with conjecture in the right way.

1. Conjecture Comes From Thirsty People

Look at chapter 17 verse 1: *"At the Lord's command, the whole community of Israel left the wilderness of Sin..."* God told the children of Israel, 'I want you to move; but I want you to move from place to place. In other words, where I am taking you will require you to make a move from your current place. You can't stay where you are if you are going to get to where I am taking you. You cannot get comfortable in any one place along the journey. I need to make sure you move from one place.' This is not Moses' doing; this is God's doing.

Another translation says they moved in stages. In other words, they had to go through different stages and phases until they arrived to the place where God wanted to take them to. God is telling them that they have only been through one stage or one phase. It's like playing a video game; you have to go through all the stages to win. And sometimes if you don't learn all you need to learn in the first stage you have to repeat that stage. Here's what God is trying to do: God is not trying to make them repeat the class. God is not trying to make them repeat the situation. He's telling them, 'This is a phase of your life so I need you Israelites to move from place to place.' Eventually, they came and "camped at Rephidim."

Rephidim means resting place. Still in verse 1, *"They camped at Rephidim but there was no water there for the people to drink."*

How in the world could God direct His people from a place where they had water to a place where they are supposed to be resting and they had no water? God brought His people to a place where there were no resources. Why in the world would God do that?

The people are thirsty. Conjecture comes from thirsty people. What are they thirsty for?

a) They are thirsty for Power. Verse 2 says, *"So once more, the people complained..."* They were professional complainers. This was not the first time they complained. This is not the first time they have been without water either. *"Once more the people complained against Moses."* Look at how they talk to Moses: *"Give us water to drink, they demanded."* As you can see the scripture does not say they asked for water. It does not say they requested some water. They are saying, 'Right now, we are in control. We're going to tell you what to do. Give us water, now.' They are ready to take over.

b) They are thirsty to be top Priority. Verse 2 continues, *"Give us water to drink!" they demanded. "Quiet!" Moses replied.* Have you ever had people to complain to you and you wanted to just tell them to 'Shut up!' Moses says, 'Quiet! I don't want to hear that anymore.' That's what my father and mother used to say: "Stop making all of that noise! Sit down somewhere. You're moving too much. You're talking too much. Sit down!"

"Moses says, Quiet! Why are you complaining against me, and why are you testing the Lord?" He says, 'I want you to understand, you're not just complaining against me; you're in a place where you are now testing God's patience. God was patient with us because He knew we had just come across the Red Sea and we had not been free that long, and God has already blessed and performed miracle after miracle to get us to this point. Now you're moving out of God's mercy into God's judgment if you're not careful about how you complain.' We never know when we come to the edge of God's mercy. God has mercy, but He says in Romans 9 that He will have mercy on whom He chooses to have mercy. God is having compassion, right now. Moses is telling them, 'You all are really getting close to the line where God's going to deal with you because of your complaining spirit.'

"Moses says, Quiet! Why are you complaining against me, and why are you testing the Lord?" That's because they are thirsty for top priority. The next verse says they are *"tormented by their thirst."* They have their own issues on the inside and *"they continued to argue with Moses."* They say, *"Why did you bring us out of Egypt? Are you trying to kill us, our children, and our livestock?"* They are trying to make themselves top priority. They are also trying to make Moses into a murderer, but it is all conjecture.

Not one time did anyone ask Moses how he was feeling or if he required assistance. Not one time did they ask Moses,

'Are you thirsty? Is your family okay? How are you doing?' When people are thirsty, conjecture occurs. People want power. They want everything to be about them. They are the emergency and everything else is secondary.

2. Conjecture Can Frustrate Good People

What do I mean by that? From verse 4 we see three ways in which conjecture can frustrate good people:

a) They Drove Moses to Prayer. Verse 4 says, *"Then Moses cried out to the Lord."* Moses is trying to grow up. He is trying to be better. He is eighty years old. He does not need to be acting like the Moses of old. Moses is leading God's people and he cries out to God in prayer. Notice this: have you ever been frustrated with some situations so much so you do not even have words to express what you're feeling? The situation is so frustrating that all you can say is, "God!" And why is it that you look up? Because you're crying out to God. Moses was so frustrated they drove him to prayer.

b) They made him desperate for a Decision. Verse 4 says, *"Then Moses cried out to the Lord, What should I do with these people?"* Notice Moses did not say, 'What shall I do with ***my*** people?' He said, 'What do I do with *these* people?' When you are tired of dealing with people, you say, 'Go get your mama. Go get your friend. Go get so-and-so.' You are thinking, 'You're acting like somebody I do not know, and right now, I am disconnecting myself from you because you are strange to me.' 'So Moses cries out, "God, what do I do with these people? I have a few ideas of what I can do to them, but these are Your people, so I want to make sure I treat Your people like You want them treated because I do not need you getting on my case because I did something wrong to them." Remember, Moses had been guilty of letting his emotions get the best of him before. At forty years of age he ended up killing somebody he was frustrated with and went on the run for another forty years. Moses said, 'I know how to get them, but I'm trying to be grown and mature now, Lord. I need to know what you want me to do with these people. I'm desperate for a decision.'

c) Moses felt the need to be Defended. Verse 4 says, *"Then Moses cried out to the Lord. What should I do with these people? They are ready to stone me."* You'd think Moses was scared of being stoned. First, Moses is eighty-years-old and is about to die anyway. Second, Moses was bold. He went down into Pharaoh's army at eighty-years-old with a stick and God. Moses was not scared; he's frustrated, and when you're frustrated, you recognize you have to call out to God and tell Him, 'I need a decision that You need me to make. I need to be protected.' Moses is not just talking about protecting himself from the people, but the people being protected from him. Moses is saying, 'Lord, I do know how to defend myself. I just don't want to defend myself like I am used to defending myself. Right now, I need You to defend me.'

Sometimes I'm not scared of what people are going to do to me. I'm scared of what I am going to do to them. I know some of you were born with a Bible and with anointing oil; but every now and then, I have to pray a little bit harder when I am dealing with certain kinds of people and certain situations. When certain things that I could do come to my mind, I have to smile to keep from looking crazy.

God says, let me show you, Moses, how to handle conjecturing people.

3. Conjecture Can't Compete With Composure

God says, 'Moses, I know they are making false accusations about you, about the situation, and about everything that's going on. What I need you to do is not act like the old you. I need you to chill and keep your composure. Moses, I need you to be calm. Don't act the fool.'

Sometimes, the Lord tells us to keep our composure. He says, 'I'm glad you cried out to Me and not to them. I need you to keep your composure because conjecture cannot compete with composure.' As a matter of fact, conjecture is frustrated by composure, so here's how you handle it:

a) Remember your Calling. Verse 5 reads, *"The Lord said to Moses, **Walk out in front of the people.**"* God tells Moses, 'All I need for you to do is to act calmly—that's how you know you are in control of a situation.' When you are hollering and screaming, you are trying to bring control back. When you're just walking out in front you're letting people know you are in control. 'Moses, I need you to keep your composure and get back to what I called you to be.

Remember, I called you to bring My children of Israel out of Egyptian bondage and take them to the Promised Land. Your calling has not changed, but because you're frustrated, you've lost your composure for a moment. Get it together, and get back in position.'

b) Remember what you're Carrying. *"The Lord said to Moses, Walk out in front of the people.* ***Take your staff,*** *the one you used when you struck the water of the Nile."* God says, 'Remember what you carry. I want you to make sure you pick up that stick that I gave you before you even dealt with Pharaoh and before you even came to this point of frustration. The people are thirsty again, and I have already given you something to help you in this situation. When you stretched that stick out over the Red Sea, the waters parted. Moses, I want you to remember that you're carrying an anointing with you.' Anointing is the ability for God to add His *super* to your *natural* so *supernatural* stuff can happen in your life. 'Moses, I want you to understand you have the super walking with your natural, and I want to make sure that you don't disconnect the two, and that you don't drop your anointing dealing with crazy people. I want to make sure you pick back up what you have because you're going to need it going forward.' Remember your calling. Remember what you are carrying.

c) Remember your Comrades. Comrades are partners, people you can trust. Verse 5 says: *"The Lord said to Moses, Walk out in front of the people. Take your staff, the one you used when you struck the water of the Nile, and* ***call some of the elders of Israel to join you."*** He did not say, call all of the elders, because as the journey keeps going, there are some folk you recognize you cannot trust at the next level. You have to know, in this season, who's just going along with you and who you can really depend on when times get hard. God says, 'Remember your comrades, Moses.'

If you keep your composure, you'll recognize what takes place when conjecture hits your life and you'll end up having the right response.

4. Composure Opens the Door to Exposure

God says, 'Moses, if you keep your composure, you're about to be exposed to some stuff you would not have been exposed to at this level. How you handle this next situation in your life depends on what you have been exposed to.' Here are three things that you will be exposed to:

a) Exposure to God's Presence. Look at verse 6: ***"I will stand before you on the rock at Mount Sinai."*** God says, 'I am going to stand in front of you if you keep your composure. I'm going to show up and you'll see Me standing in front of you on the rock. You're going to see My presence.'

b) Exposure to your Power. Verse 6 continues, *"I will stand before you on the rock at Mount Sinai;* ***strike the rock.****"* Moses is in a situation where he is frustrated and he feels powerless to make the right decision and that's why he is crying out to God. So God says, 'Moses, you are in a situation where, although you feel powerless, you have more power than you think. When My presence shows up, you're going to be exposed to your power. I want you to take your stick, and I want you to strike the rock. I know you're frustrated, and when you're frustrated you have to alleviate some of your frustration. I want you to swing at what's in front of you. I do not want you to strike the people; that is your flesh that is wanting to do this. I want you to use your faith. I don't need you in your flesh because I know what you could do with that stick if you don't keep your composure. Right now, you might turn around and strike a whole lot of them with that stick. I don't need for you to do that. I need you to keep your composure, and when you keep your composure, you're going to see My presence, then you're going to see that you have more power than you think you have.'

c) Exposure to God's Provision. Verse 6 says, *"I will stand before you on the rock at Mount Sinai, strike the rock,* ***and water will come gushing out****, then the people will be able to drink. So Moses struck the rock as he was told, and water gushed out as the elders looked on."* Now, look at what Moses did after this: He saw what had taken place; he did what God called him to do in the midst of all this conjecture, and verse 7 tells us he *"named the place Massah, which means test, and Meribah, which means arguing. Because the people of Israel argued with Moses and tested the Lord by simply saying, Is the Lord here with us or not?"*

Moses is saying, 'Alright, I see water flowing, but I didn't need the water to flow for me. You don't see me arguing or complaining on this journey. Why am I not acting like you all? Because I know the Lord is here with us. How do I know the Lord is here with us? Because I've been talking with Him and He's the one who designed the route for us in the first place. And since He is the one who designed the route for us, why do you all think He would deliver us from Egypt to die at Rephidim? He won't do that. I've been having conversations with Him, therefore, I don't have to engage in conjecture about what God is going to do because He's already told me what He will do.' When you keep good company with God, God begins to give you information about what is going to take place next. Even if He does not give you all the details, He'll give you peace in your spirit that everything He says will come to pass.

Moses says, 'Now, Israelites, can't you all look back and see how many times God has already opened up the door, how many times God has already blessed, how many times God has already helped us through a situation? Why would God leave us now in the midst of this place where we're supposed to be resting? God is the one who never sleeps nor slumbers. Why are we up arguing and fussing and fighting? I know you don't have what you need right now, but if God brought you here, God can keep you in the place He brought you.'

Are you dealing with conjecture in your life? Conjecture comes from thirsty people around you. They are thirsty for power, for control, and to be top priority. If they are not thirsty for those three things, they might be thirsty for your life. People who talk about your life all the time show that they do not have a life. Whenever you do not have a life, you spend your time looking at everybody else's life and talking them down. You don't have to be thirsty about anybody because you are not the woman at the well. You are not showing up trying to get physical water when you already have a touch of the spiritual water.

Let me tell you what the spiritual water is: it is when you have been born again, baptized, saved and filled with the Holy Ghost. Jesus said if you have a drink, you'll never have to drink again. I am talking about internal security — knowing who you are. And no matter who you are, if you are working at McDonald's, you still know that you are first class. If you're on an airplane and they sit you by the engine, you're still first class. First class is not where you sit; first class is Who is on the inside of you. *"Greater is He who is in me."* When you are dealing with thirsty people that is a sign that you are full of something God wants to happen. If you don't know that you are full just raise your hands and say, 'Fill my cup, Lord. Fill it up, Lord.' God wants to fill your cup and fill your life because you're dealing with thirsty people.

Not only should you know that conjecture comes from the thirsty people in your life, but you should know that the conjecture of others can leave you feeling frustrated. You may be saying, 'I'm trying to grow spiritually. It used to be where I didn't call on God first; I would call on the Smith and Wesson.' You might be saying, 'I have never had a fight in my life. I'm not big enough to fight, but if you could read what's going on inside of my head, you'd think I could be a serial killer. I'm trying to make sure I go to God in prayer. I have to get on my knees every now and then. When I get on my knees, I end up changing my perspective. I end up getting out of my flesh and getting into my faith.'

Perhaps, right now, you are in a desperate situation. You don't want to make the wrong decision about your co-worker. You have kids to feed. You have a car note to pay. You don't want to make the wrong decision about a family member. You don't want to make the wrong decision about your marriage. You want to make sure you don't make a personal decision out of your emotions. You want to be led by the Spirit.

Are you tired of making decisions on your own? If so, then you have to clean up what you have messed up and go and get right with God. Talk your frustrations out with God. Do like the Psalmist who said, "I look to the hills from whence cometh my help; my help comes from the Lord."

Every now and then, you will feel like you need somebody to defend you because you want to defend everybody else. Sometimes when you need to be defended, nobody will stand up for you; it will seem like everybody is against you.

If you do what God says to do, the Bible says in Romans 8:31, "*If God is for us* (you) *who can be against us* (you)*?*" He is more than who can be against you. Realize that you have backup. You have the Father, the Son, and the Holy Ghost. You may not be aware of it, but there is somebody praying for you. The angels of the Lord are encamped around you all night and all day. So don't worry, don't act stupid, get yourself together, straighten up your mind, and keep your composure. That will keep your flesh in check.

Do you have an alter ego? Then, don't pull up the wrong

person. You may pull up the person who may not be as saved as you are now. Even though I am saved, I am not fully delivered yet. I still have to pray a little bit more. I still have to watch myself. I love Jesus, but I will defend myself at all cost. If you mess with my family, I will defend them. If you mess with my children, I will defend them. If you mess with my money, I will defend myself, but, if you mess with my God, He will defend Himself.

Keep your composure and remember what God called you to do. When you know who you are, you won't have to keep telling people who the boss is. You don't have to keep telling people you're the man. You are what you are; just walk it out and everybody will see that you have the power to overcome anything. How do I know? Because in Psalm 23:4, "David didn't say yea though I run or skip through, he said yea though I walk through the valley of the shadow of death, I will fear no evil."

Composure will open up doors you have never seen before. People wouldn't be talking about you if you didn't have anything going for you. They wouldn't be talking if you weren't about anything. If they are talking about you, it simply means that they are in the audience and you are on the stage. Give them the best show they have ever seen in their life.

One week, when our new church building was under construction, people were stopping by and looking. Some were wondering if we were going to be ready by a certain date. There was stuff on the floor and stuff hanging from the ceiling, but I was not nervous because while they were looking at a pile, I was looking at progress. While they were looking at plain walls, I was envisioning the painted walls in my head. While they were looking at what seemed dark, I was already seeing the lights on. I was not nervous because I had been talking with the contractor and the city manager about the project. I knew what their plans were going forward. I had also been talking with the Head of the church—Jesus. While others were nervous, I was praising God. I did not have to be nervous because I was seeing things that the onlookers were not seeing.

You may be looking at your bills when you ought to be looking at your blessings. The reason why you have bills is because God has created some money somewhere for you to pay those bills. God will never take you to a place where He cannot keep you. You might be looking at a divorce when you should be looking at deliverance. You might be looking at a lay-off when you should be looking at an opportunity for God to open up another door.

While Jesus was hanging on the cross, many people walked by and they saw defeat, but Jesus was looking at deliverance. He knew that all power in Heaven and earth was in His hands. The situation did not look like what it really was. While He was on the cross, He said, "It is finished." His purpose for the cross was finished. The purpose for which He came to earth was finished. However, early Sunday morning, He rose with all power in His hands.

Don't mix up what has happened or is happening to you now with what God has for you in the future. Your pain, your problems, and your negative experiences may be finished, but God is not finished with you. In fact, He may just be getting started. He has blessings, joy, and deliverance coming your way.

At the Lord's command, the whole community of Israel left the wilderness of Sin and moved from place to place. Eventually they camped at Rephidim, but there was no water there for the people to drink. So once more the people complained against Moses. "Give us water to drink!" they demanded.

"Quiet!" Moses replied. "Why are you complaining against me? And why are you testing the Lord?"

But tormented by thirst, they continued to argue with Moses. "Why did you bring us out of Egypt? Are you trying to kill us, our children, and our livestock with thirst?"

Then Moses cried out to the Lord, "What should I do with these people? They are ready to stone me!"

The Lord said to Moses, "Walk out in front of the people. Take your staff, the one you used when you struck the water of the Nile, and call some of the elders of Israel to join you. I will stand before you on the rock at Mount Sinai. Strike the rock, and water will come gushing out. Then the people will be able to drink." So Moses struck the rock as he was told, and water gushed out as the elders looked on.

Moses named the place Massah (which means “test”) and Meribah (which means “arguing”) because the people of Israel argued with Moses and tested the Lord by saying, “Is the Lord here with us or not?”

Exodus 17:1-7 (NLT)

Focus Verse: Verse 3: “But tormented by thirst, they continued to argue with Moses, why did you bring us out of Egypt? Are you trying to kill us, our children, and our livestock with thirst?

9

Expect Companionship When You're in Transition

Finding out what is next in moving from dreams to reality in fulfilling the assignment God has for our lives causes us to have to go through seasons of transition. As we look at the seasons of transition, we see that there are several things we must experience. Following the journey of the Israelites after their deliverance from slavery in Egypt, we have looked at how they went through the following: changes, challenges, a character check, code compliance, complaining, confirmation, conflict, and conjecture.

Moses had a tough time as the leader of the Israelites. Even though he had many people around him, he may have felt as though he was along. First, he had the congregation: these are the people he had to lead. Then, we saw that he had some comrades: Aaron and Hur, for example, who held up his hands, as well as Joshua who fought for him. We see from the passage above that God, in His wisdom, saw that Moses needed not just comrades, but companionship. When we are in times of transition, we need companionship as well.

The Collins English Dictionary defines *companionship* as "having someone you know and like with you." It's not just having someone you know, but also having someone you like. How many people do you know who you do not like? There is a difference with someone just being *in* a marriage with you as opposed to someone *being* married to you. Some spouses are not soul-mates, but cell-mates.

Let's talk about companionship, not just in marriage, but in every level of life. God looked at Adam and said, 'You know what, Adam? It's not good for man to be alone.' In other words, there are some needs that God will not meet. There are some things God won't do. Loneliness shows up in different ways. If God wanted us to be by ourselves, then He would have created each of us and placed us by ourselves and He would have just left us alone; but that's not how God created us. He created us for companionship. When I talk about companionship, I'm not saying that everybody ought to be married, because God did not promise everybody they would be married. He does desire that everybody be a companion to somebody else. He desires that everybody has somebody they like—somebody they can live life with. Friends, relatives, associates—anybody—can be a companion.

God tells Adam, 'I'm going to meet your spiritual needs, but I'm going to create somebody else who will meet your physical needs.' Adam needed Eve emotionally and physically. God created her to be a help-meet—a helper to Adam. I've said this a million times: if you're going to have somebody in your life, then that person needs to be able to do something. If they are doing nothing, then you don't need their help to do nothing. Eve was to bring help to Adam. They were to be companions in the Garden.

At this stage, in Moses' transitional period with the children of Israel, we see that he needed some companionship. He did not need somebody in his life to take life from him, but somebody in his life to do life with him. Everybody in his life, up to that point, was taking life from him. Everybody was getting something from him. The people he was leading were constantly complaining. He could not treat them as companions; he had to play a certain role with them. He already had a calling on his life. He had success. He had comrades, but he needed someone tailor-made for him at this stage in his life journey.

God was very gracious to Moses. He did not just give him one companion. According to our reading of the scriptures, God gave Moses four people who were companions to him. Remember, a companion is not just somebody who you are married to; it's somebody who you like and somebody who you can do life with. Here we have four different people and they brought four different things in Moses' life that he needed. The four people are Jethro, Zipporah, Gershom, and Eliezer.

In verse 1 of chapter 18 we read: *"Moses' father-in-law, Jethro, priest of Midian, heard about everything God had done for*

Moses and his people the Israelites. He heard especially about how the Lord had rescued them from out of Egypt."

Earlier, Moses had sent his wife and his two sons back to Jethro who had taken them in. Moses had been leading the children of Israel and leading them well. Leading them had been a frustrating situation. It didn't matter if they liked him; it didn't matter if they loved him. God had given him an assignment and his assignment, whether they liked it or not, was to help get them to where they needed to be. Don't get your assignment in someone else's life mixed up with companionship. Your relationship with some people will be a job, a duty.

God stands by those whom He calls into leadership. However, even strong people, often feel distraught, broken, and lonely. However, because they are used to putting on their strong face, everybody else whom they are helping feels that they are alright.

If you have been called into leadership, your followers will always expect you to be okay. There are two reasons for this: One, you have proven yourself to be able to stand alone and help many others. The second reason is that you have been faking for so long that you don't know how to be vulnerable and let somebody know you are hurting because you have too much pride to tell somebody you need them to pray for you. Usually, when you are not vulnerable and you refuse to let people know you really need help, you end up being resentful against others because nobody prayed for you. Well, are you acting as though you don't need any help?

Don't let your pride keep you lonely. Don't let your

pride keep you from letting people help you. There is no point in acting as though all is well when you are really broken.

Back to Moses: He is in the wilderness, and he is also in a wild place in his life. He's in a transition period. God says, 'I have to send Moses some reinforcements. I have to send somebody who's not a job for you, somebody who does not see you as a bank, someone who does not see you as someone to get by on. I need to send companionship.'

Jethro

The first person we see here is Jethro. Jethro was ***a source of connection***. Moses needed somebody to be a source of connection. He needed a companion who could make some connections in his life for him. He needed somebody who knew how to network for him. Everybody needs somebody who has relationships and people skills. How did Jethro fulfill this role as a connector?

a) He Connected Moses with his wife. When Moses was over forty years old and he ran away from Pharaoh's place because he killed someone. He ran to Midian where he ended up getting married after he defended the seven daughters of Jethro. These seven sisters were being taunted by others when Moses met them. (Remember, Moses had just finished killing someone, and you don't want to mess with somebody when he is in a killing mode.) Moses delivered the sisters from the men who were harassing them. When Jethro heard about it, he said, 'Man, I have to thank you. You can marry my daughter, Zipporah.' So, Jethro was a source of connection.

b) He Reconnected Moses in transition with his family. Verse 5 says, *"Jethro, Moses' father-in-law, now came to visit Moses in the wilderness; he brought Moses' wife and two sons with him."* Jethro's name means friend of God. It is good to be friends with somebody who is a friend of God, because if they are a friend of God, they are going to seek God in your life. They are going to help you do what God has called you to do. They are going to be a friend to the ministry of God. They are going to be a friend to the purposes of God.

When Moses was called to deliver the Israelites, the whole family was called to ministry. Moses was about to go and do the assignment that God has chosen him for, and en route to Egypt, some things happen. For one thing, his wife and sons do not make it into Egypt. Moses actually sent them back to his father-in-law.

Jethro was a priest in Midian. Your Bible commentary will tell you that Midian was nowhere near Africa, but that's not really true. They try to put it in a place called the Middle East. The Midianites are the Cushites. If you know who the Cushites are then you might know who the Kennites are. The Kennites are the Ethiopians. The last time I checked, Ethiopia is a country on the continent of Africa. What I am trying to tell you is this: the person who God is bringing as a companion into Moses' life is not a blood relative. Everyone who is a part of your family will not necessarily be a companion; likewise, all of your companions will not necessarily be blood relatives. God can introduce you to somebody who is totally unrelated to you when you are in transition in your own life.

That is how Moses ended up meeting his father-in-law.

So, we see that Jethro was a source of connection: he connected Moses with his wife and he reconnected Moses with his family while Moses was in transition. While Moses is stuck in the wilderness, tired, busted, and disgusted, Jethro is in Midian saying to his daughter, 'You know what? We need to go pay your honey a visit. I need to go pay my son-in-law a visit.'

Zipporah

The second person who came into Moses' life was Zipporah. **Zipporah provided the service of comfort.** How did she provide a service of comfort? She did this in three ways.

Verse 5 says, *"Jethro, Moses' father-in-law, now came to visit Moses in the wilderness; he brought Moses' wife and two sons with him."* They had been disconnected at least two months. Moses had been separated from his family doing what God called him to do, and there is no drama. When you have a calling on your life, you have to recognize that when God calls you then God calls you and nobody else. That is why, when you get married, the person you get hooked up with is on loan to you. They are not yours. When God wants to use them, He will come and get them. You might be jealous, but you are not more jealous than God. God can call you or your spouse at any time.

As a companion, Zipporah provided a service of comfort by...

a) Her Presence. Moses was forty and on the run from Pharaoh when he met and married Zipporah, but now 80 years old, he needs her in his life now more than ever. They reconnect when he's on the run to his destiny. He says, 'Baby, I was running from something when I met you, but now I need to run with you to where God is trying to take me.' Her presence made a difference because he now has his running buddy.

There is nothing like having somebody who will just run with you. You don't have to ask a bunch of questions. You don't have to wonder what their motives are. Their presence just makes a difference. Zipporah's presence brought comfort to Moses because he knew where her heart was.

b) Her Passion. In Exodus chapter 4, we see Zipporah's passion on display. God called Moses, 'Moses, go down and tell Pharaoh to let My people go.' They pack their belongings. They get ready to leave for Egypt. Zipporah's passion brought Moses comfort because she fought for him and now she fought with him. From Exodus chapter 4, we see where Moses had to be circumcised and his children had to be circumcised as well, because when God looked down and saw circumcision, He said, 'Those are My covenant people.'

Well, on their way to Egypt, Moses' sons had not been circumcised. God said, 'Moses, you have not circumcised your sons yet. I am going to kill you.' God was serious about circumcision. Moses became stricken with an illness. He was about to die because he would not circumcise his sons. Zipporah grabbed a flint knife, cut it off, and threw it at the feet of Moses. Moses was able to say, 'I am thankful you are in my life,' because she had a passion for him. She said, 'God, don't kill him; he's just a little slow right now.'

Moses was thankful that his wife saved his life. She fought for him. She talked to God. She interceded on behalf of the one she loved. She was a true companion; sometimes sisters have to step up when brothers are not acting right.

She did not just fight for him; she fought with him. After she did that, verse 25 goes on to say: "Now you are a bridegroom of blood to me." In other words, 'You are a bloody sacrifice.' Nobody really knows what that means, but what our Bible commentators are clear on is that it was not nice. It seemed like she had an attitude. She felt she had to circumcise her own children, which her husband, as the leader of the home, should have done himself. Her behavior from some scholars may be one of not wanting to take on the religion of Moses or its practice of circumcision. So, this from one viewpoint is her act of disgust in circumcision having to be performed on her child.

Zipporah fought for Moses and she fought with Moses. How in the world did that bring Moses comfort? A real man wants a woman in his life who is not just going to let him do anything when she knows he is wrong. She is not just going to go along to get along. Before they get married, some men ought to ask their potential spouse: Can you fight the devil off me? Can you fight in prayer? Can you talk to God when I am not doing right? If the answer is, "Yes," that brings comfort to that man. It brings comfort to a brother to know that if he steps out of line he has somebody who won't just have his back in his face, but will have it behind his back.

Her presence. Her passion. And now ...

c) Her Parenting brought him comfort. Look at verse: *"Jethro, Moses' father-in-law...brought Moses' wife and two sons with him and they arrived where Moses and the people were camped near the mountain of God."* Why does her parenting bring him comfort? Because Moses had enough confidence in the woman he had children with to know that when he goes and handles business, when he comes back, his sons will be alright.

Zipporah's parenting skills end up bringing Moses comfort because he knows he could do his job and come home and everything would be alright. We don't see the children, his sons, having any kind of identity crisis. We don't see them having any kind of problems. They just show up and, apparently, everything is alright.

Jethro was a source of connection. Zipporah provided the service of comfort with her presence, her passion, and her parenting skills. You may still be wondering: How did she provide a source of comfort? Let's look at what her name means as well. Zipporah's name means little bird. Often, in the Old Testament, we find that people are named according to their personality or accomplishments. Zipporah brought comfort just by showing up, and what came out of her mouth were gentle chirps. Zipporah was a gentle, comforting influence in Moses' life.

Gershom

Jethro was a source of connection. Zipporah provided the service of comfort. Gershom, Moses' first son *humbled him with a sense of compassion.* Gershom's name means foreigner. Looking at verse 5 once more, we read *"Jethro, Moses' father-in-law, now came to visit Moses in the wilderness; he brought Moses' wife and two sons with him and they arrived where Moses and the people were camped near the mountain of God."* Looking at verse 3, we want to see what Gershom brought to the table as a way of companionship. Moses' first son was named Gershom, because, when he was born, Moses said *"I have been a foreigner in a foreign land."*

Gershom humbled Moses with a sense of compassion. This is a companion, a son, who came into his life and who ends up causing Moses to become humble. You need somebody in your life who will cause you to become humble whenever you see them. There are three ways in which Gershom caused Moses to be more humble and compassionate.

1) He reminded him of his Past. Gershom reminded Moses, 'Moses, don't forget where you came from. You haven't always been eighty-years-old leading people out of Israel. No, you were born and actually put in a basket in order to survive. You were born a Hebrew in Egypt—a foreigner.' When Moses named his son, Gershom, he said, 'I'm going to name you foreigner because you're going to remind me where I came from.' And now in this season in the wilderness, Moses looks at his son and says, 'You know what? You remind me of where I came from.' You need people in your life who will say to you, 'You ain't all that now. Remember where you came from.'

Not just that, but Gershom

2) Reminded him of his Pain. Moses was raised as an Egyptian; but the older he became, he started learning who he really was—a Hebrew. And when he found out who he really was, he didn't want to see an Egyptian hurt his Hebrew people. So, what did he do? He ended up doing the wrong thing. He tried to deliver the Hebrew man, but he ends up killing an Egyptian too. So he says, 'Whenever I look at you, Gershom, I'm reminded of my past, but I'm also reminded of my pain because it reminds me that my people were suffering and I couldn't do anything about it. As a matter of fact, I tried to help, but I helped the wrong way. You remind me of the pain that I carried for so many years. You remind me of my past, but, oh, thank God, when I look at you Gershom, you...

3) Remind me of my Purpose.' Moses' name means to draw out, and he was born to deliver God's people. G od called him to draw them out. As a matter of fact, when Moses was born, he, too, needed to be rescued. What happened during his childhood was a part of his purpose. Don't curse your childhood; God was using that to help you with your purpose. If you ever want to know what your real purpose is, go research your pain and the thing that hurt you the most will often be the thing that God uses to point out your purpose. What you went through will enable you to minister to others who went through similar situations. Help others go through that situation. Who else can be humble enough and have compassion other than somebody who went through it too? Gershom reminded Moses of his past, of the pain that he experienced, and of the purpose which he was now fulfilling.

Jethro was a source of connection. Zipporah provided the service of comfort. Gershom humbled Moses with a sense of compassion. Now we come to the fourth person in Moses' life during this time of transition—Eliezer.

Eliezer

Eliezer gave Moses *strength to stand with courage*. Verse 4 of our scripture reading states: *"His second son was named Eliezer, for Moses had said, the God of my ancestors was my helper. He rescued me from the sword of Pharaoh."* Eliezer's name means God is my helper. He gives Moses courage when Moses sees his face. Moses says, here's a companion in my life, therefore, I'm going to have courage. Someone once said this about courage: "Courage doesn't always roar. Sometimes courage is the quiet voice at the end of the day that says: We'll try again tomorrow." Sometimes courage isn't about broadcasting your business and looking all tough. Sometimes courage is: 'I'm waking up another day.' Just because you're not loud with it that does not mean you are not courageous.

If you showed up for church one more time, you have courage. You told the devil, 'You thought you had me yesterday, but I'm coming back with another fight, another swing. I'm coming back to the ring right now.' Eliezer gave

Moses strength to stand with courage because Moses needed courage as it seemed like everybody and everything were against him, but he kept on going.

Moses was reminded of who had helped him in the past. He named his kids when he was forty years old, after he had run from Pharaoh, and ended up marrying Zipporah. The first one he named 'foreigner' because he reminded him of where he came from. He named the second one 'the only reason I escaped was because God was my helper.'

I thank God for verse 4, because what this scripture teaches is that there are not just generational curses; there are also generational blessings. Moses said, "*the God of my ancestors has helped me.*" In other words, Moses is saying, 'I did not get where I am by myself; I came here because God is not new to helping people in my family.' Perhaps you can look back over your family line and say, 'God has been helping my family for a long time.' Much of where you are today can be attributed to parents, grandparents, and great-grandparents who prayed, attended church, were faithful to God, and, thus, obtained God's blessings and help. You are the beneficiary of blessings that you did not even pray for because somebody else back in your family line was faithful to God. God is an ancestry-blessing God. Thank God that He placed some folks in your life who knew how to build you up. They brought encouragement into your life. They brought strength into your life. They brought companionship into your life.

God sent true companionship into Moses' life. These people did not want anything from him, they just wanted him to be better. They just wanted to be in his presence, and he wanted to be in their presence. After Jethro provided connection, Zipporah provided comfort, Gershom provided compassion, and Eliezer provided courage, they created in Moses a reason for celebration.

A Reason for Celebration

Moses probably has not smiled since Exodus 15. What he has been called to do has worn on him so much, and he did not have anybody in his life to pour into him. If you do not pray for anything else, pray that God would send some people who can give you something and not just take from you. That is companionship. Moses has not cracked a smile since the Israelites came across the Red Sea and wrote that song; that was the last time we saw Moses singing. After that, everybody in his life is unhappy with how he has been acting. Everybody else in his life is only happy with him when he does something for them. Can you imagine what your life would be like if the only time people in your life are happy with you is when you give them something or do something for them?

You shouldn't get companionship mixed up with your assignment toward people. Some people you are called to lead; others you can actually be a companion to. You cannot be a companion to everyone under your leadership. You have to know where to draw the line with the people you deal with even in the church. Everyone in the church cannot be your buddy. The proper companion-ships will not be a drag on you; they will create in you a reason to celebrate

Jethro, Zipporah, Gershom, and Eliezer gave Moses three causes for celebration:

1) Conversation. Verse 7 says: *"Moses went out to meet with his father-in-law, he bowed low and kissed him; they asked about each other's welfare and then went into Moses' tent. Moses told his father-in-law everything that the Lord had done to Pharaoh and Egypt on behalf of Israel."* Men do talk. They just stop talking when they get interrupted or judged. This confirms that Moses told Jethro everything.

2) Compassion. Moses now has somebody he can talk to who is not trying to judge him or find fault with what he is saying or doing. Probably for the first time in a long time, he can openly share with somebody. That is what a companion will allow you to do. The conversation is engaging because Moses and Jethro are conversing as equals. With a true companion, you will not feel like you are under arrest or on the witness stand during a conversation.

Verses 9-11 read, *"Jethro was delighted when he heard about all the good things the Lord had done for Israel. And how he rescued them from the hand of the Egyptians."* Jethro was excited about Moses' success. Have you ever talked with someone and they are happy for you until you tell them too much and you begin to feel as though they are getting jealous? Moses could keep conversing with Jethro because he was talking to a companion who was secure within themselves. Jethro could handle Moses' blessings.

Looking at verse 10, we see how Jethro responds: *"Praise the Lord!"* Jethro says, 'I am going to praise the Lord with you.' *"For he has rescued you from the Egyptians and from the hand of Pharaoh; yes, he has rescued Israel from the powerful hand of Egypt."*

3) With his Companion, Moses showed God some appreciation. In verses 11-12, Jethro says, *"I know now that the Lord is greater than all the other gods because he rescued his people from the oppression of the proud Egyptians. Then Jethro, Moses' father-in-law, brought a burnt offering and sacrifices to God, and Aaron and all the elders of Israel came out and joined him in a sacrificial meal in God's presence."* They fellowshiped; they sat down; they broke bread together. When you have somebody who is a companion in your life—a friend, a brother, a sister, a mate, or somebody you are with—they will pour into your life. They won't drain your life. They will build you up, not tear you down. They are not perfect, but they are perfect for you.

Jesus is the greatest companion you could ever have. He says, 'I lived, I died, I rose again for you.' And He invites us to have a relationship with Him—to be co-laborers with Him. We can talk with Jesus and not feel judged. He will pour into us; He will correct us; He will strengthen us; He will give us courage.

Moses' father-in-law, Jethro, the priest of Midian, heard about everything God had done for Moses and his people, the Israelites. He heard especially about how the Lord had rescued them from Egypt.

Earlier, Moses had sent his wife, Zipporah, and his two sons back to Jethro, who had taken them in.

(Moses' first son was named Gershom, for Moses had said when the boy was born, "I have been a foreigner in a foreign land." His second son was named Eliezer, for Moses had said, "The God of my ancestors was my helper; he rescued me from the sword of Pharaoh.") Jethro, Moses' father-in-law, now came to visit Moses in the wilderness. He brought Moses' wife and two sons with him, and they arrived while Moses and the people were camped near the mountain of God. Jethro had sent a message to Moses, saying, "I, Jethro, your father-in-law, am coming to see you with your wife and your two sons."

So Moses went out to meet his father-in-law. He bowed low and kissed him. They asked about each other's welfare and then went into Moses' tent. Moses told his father-in-law everything the Lord had done to Pharaoh and Egypt on behalf of Israel. He also told about all the hardships they had experienced along the way and how the Lord had rescued his people from all their troubles. Jethro was delighted when he heard about all the good things the Lord had done for Israel as he rescued them from the hand of the Egyptians.

"Praise the Lord," Jethro said, "for he has rescued you from the Egyptians and from Pharaoh. Yes, he has rescued Israel from the powerful hand of Egypt! I know now that the Lord is greater than all other gods, because he rescued his people from the oppression of the proud Egyptians."

Then Jethro, Moses' father-in-law, brought a burnt offering and sacrifices to God. Aaron and all the elders of Israel came out and joined him in a sacrificial meal in God's presence.

Exodus 18:1-12 (NLT)

Focus Verse: Verse 5: "Jethro, Moses' father-in-law, now came to visit Moses in the wilderness and he brought Moses' wife and two sons with him and they arrived where Moses and the people were camped near the mountain of God."

10

Expect Communication When You're in Transition

To end our discussion on things to expect when you're in transition, we must be reminded that transitions in life are necessary. If we want to go where God wants us to go transition is mandatory. We cannot stay where we want to stay; we cannot be comfortable where we want to be comfortable. There is a place where God has designed and destined for us to go in our lives. As we study the journey of the Israelites out of Egypt, we see how God has worked through their lives and has taken them through multiple transitions. In this last chapter, I present to you the tenth thing to expect when we are in transition, and that is, we are to expect communication.

The Israelites are en route from Egyptian bondage to the Promised Land. They still have not arrived as of yet at the place where God has destined them to go. They are still in motion, still in transition on their way to where God has destined them to be. However, they are closer to their destiny than they have ever been before. Through all the transitions that you have been through in life, you are closer to your destiny than you've ever been before. You may not be where you want to be, but you can thank God that you are not where you used to be.

That is where the children of Israel are right now. They are making progress; they are making strides. They have already gone through nine stages of transition:

1) *Changes*
2) *Challenges*
3) *Character Check*
4) *Code Compliance*
5) *Complaining*
6) *Confirmation*
7) *Conflict*
8) *Conjecture*
9) *Companionship*

Before we get into our tenth transitional expectation, let's look at Exodus 18:13 where we will recognize an expectation of *coaching* through transition. Moses needed some coaching; he needed some mentoring as he went through the process of leadership, so God ended up sending Jethro. We all need a Jethro in our lives. You need a Jethro when, despite your education and experience, you come to a place in your life where you recognize that you are doing more than you were doing before and you are doing more than was expected of you, and you begin to get overwhelmed. Then, you realize that somebody has been where you are right now. That person is your Jethro.

Jethro says, 'Listen, you need somebody to come into your life to teach you a new strategy, because the strategy you used to get here is not going to be the strategy you use to get to where you're going. You're going to have to learn to trust more people because you're going to minimize the big vision God gave you to something you can manage. If you minimize God's dream, you end up choking your own dreams.' When God gives you a dream, He pushes you to a point where you end up saying to yourself, 'I don't know how I am going to do this.' And when you end up saying that, you realize that the dream God gave you is bigger than what you can accomplish on your own. Thus, you need a dream team. You need people around you who can understand the dream, who can understand the strategy, and who will help you make sure that the dream comes to pass.

You need a Jethro who can coach you because Jethro has experience and wisdom. You might not even have a physical Jethro—maybe you have a book, a class, or a seminar from which you can learn. Whatever the case, know that, if God calls you, God will also equip you. The question is, are you humble enough to sit and listen to somebody pour into you? Or do you think that what has brought you this far can take you to where you need to be? If you think that, you will struggle the rest of the way. So, you need to expect and embrace coaching while you are in transition.

Communication

Now we come to one of the most vital parts that will make or break any situation. It will help or hurt any relationship that you have. That's communication. From the journey out of Egypt with the children of Israel, there were four forms of communication: communication between God and Moses, communication between Moses and the people, communication between the people and Moses, and communication between God and everybody. The reason communication occurred in this manner is because there were four things that needed to be understood during this time. There was communication because:

1) Something needed to be received.
2) Something needed to be expressed.
3) Somebody needed to be blessed by something.
4) They all needed to experience something.

There was communication between God, Moses, and the people at various levels. Let's look at three things that Moses ended up dealing with and at a fourth thing, which is an overflow of what took place because of those first three things.

1. Moses Received an Impartation

In verse 1, we read, *"Exactly two months after the Israelites left Egypt they arrived in the wilderness of Sinai, after breaking camp at Rephidim, they came to the wilderness of Sinai and set up camp there at the base of Mount Sinai."*

The children of Israel have just left one wilderness and are now closer than they have ever been to their destination. Now it is very, very important that they follow directions going forward, because if they don't follow directions, they are going to end up taking longer to get to their destination. They must pay attention and follow every single step that God tells them to do. If they do not, they will miss what God wants to do for them and delay their own season. It will not be the devil's fault; it will not be the enemy's fault; it will be their own fault because they did not listen to and do what God called them to do.

In the midst of that wilderness, Moses receives an impartation. Impartation means to make known, to tell, to relate, or to disclose. God is about to impart something into Moses; He's about to tell Moses what He wants to share with His people. God says, 'Moses, I'm about to tell you something that is on My heart; something that is the desire of My heart; something that I want My people to be a part of. I want them to partner with Me on this, but I'm going to impart it into you because I need to make sure you get it yourself.'

Verse 3 says, *"Then Moses climbed the mountain to appear before God; the Lord called to him from the mountain and said..."* Moses leaves the crowd and climbs the mountain by himself. Often, we cannot hear God clearly because we hang with the crowd too much, and we don't isolate ourselves with God. Maybe God is saying to you, 'I want some alone time with you in this season. I am about to tell you something that I have never told you before; I am about to share something I have never shared before. Can you disconnect yourself from the crowd? I am calling you out. Can you stand alone for a moment and hang with Me in solitude while I share something with you?'

Moses had to crawl and climb to get into God's presence, because you don't just rush into God's presence. God is everywhere present, but if you want the raw manifestation of God, you have to get in position; you have to crawl to that place; you have to fight to get to that place. You have to be higher, and thus, leave some stuff on the ground. You have to isolate yourself.

Moses gets to the mountain and he climbs to the place where he is to meet God. God says to him, 'The first thing I want you to remind the Israelites of is...'

a) How God Defended them. Verse 4 says, *"You have seen what I did to the Egyptians."* I want you to remind My people of how I defended them. I want them to remember how I stood up and defeated their enemies: how I defeated those who were trying to tear them down, scandalize their name, kill them, and destroy them. Don't forget what I did on their behalf.

b) How God Delivered them. Verse 4 continues, *"You know how I carried you on eagle's wings and brought you to myself."* God said, 'Not only did I defeat your enemies, but I didn't leave you where you were. I became like an eagle swooping down, picking you up on my pinions and then I brought you to Myself. I never deliver anybody and not desire them to be closer to Me. As a matter of fact, every deliverance is a deliverance closer to Me.' God loves close proximity. He wanted to bring His people closer to Him. He did not want them to get confused thinking He delivered them just to deliver them. He delivered them for closeness, for intimacy. God craves intimacy with all His people.

c) What God's Desire is for them. Verse 5 says: *"If you will obey Me and keep My covenant you will be My own special treasure from among all the peoples of the earth for all the earth belongs to Me. You will be My kingdom of priests; My holy nation: this is the message you must give the people of Israel."* That is a conditional promise: if you do this, this is what you will become. If you do this, you will be this. God says, 'Whatever you want to be in this life is dependent on what you do when I tell you to do it. It is if this...then that.' You will have to take responsibility for how your life turns out in your next season, but God wants you to have the best.

God's purpose for His people is for them to be His "special treasure from among all the people of the earth." God tells Moses, 'I'm going to put a special anointing on their life and they are going to be different from everybody around them. They will not fit in with everybody and they have to be able to handle that because they are going to be a special treasure. They will have to be obedient, make sacrifices, and listen to Me.'

Everyone has options in life, and blessings only come to those who obey, honor, and serve God. God wants His people to be His priests, His representatives, who live on another level because they are special to God. God tells His people, 'I desire you to not expect Me to let you get away with what your neighbor gets away with. You're different. I'm going to be harder on you. You have more favor on you.' He wants us to be the same. He wants us to be His special treasures, but we must obey and honor Him above all.

If you are a leader in transition—whether a leader of a family, church, a ministry, or otherwise—God wants to impart this message to you as well. But, it is not only for you, it is for you to share with the people around you.

2. He Delivered an Exhortation

After Moses received an impartation, he delivered an exhortation. An exhortation means an utterance or discourse; it is to convey urgent advice. When the impartation that Moses received from God leaves his lips, it becomes an exhortation. God imparts; Moses exhorts. Moses tells the people, 'God told me this, and it's urgent that you pay attention and listen to what God is saying.'

There are three things Moses did to deliver this exhortation:

a) Moses Returned to a Meeting. Verse 7 says, *"So Moses returned from the mountain and called together the elders of the people and told them everything the Lord had commanded them."* When you're exhorting you have to make sure you're exhorting the right group of people. If you don't, you're going to cast pearls before swine. God does not want you to waste His Word on people who will not listen or pay attention, so it's up to you to understand who you have around you.

God says, 'Alright, I have an assignment. You are going to the Promised Land. I already told you I told Jethro to tell you to change your strategy. I want you to put some men over thousands, some over fifties, and some over hundreds. These men have influence and they will help you manage the people going forward. I'm imparting to you, but now I need you to go and exhort those people who I chose to be next to you. These are the people who you will choose. These are the people with the right kind of spirit and mindset. You should be on one accord. They should have a heart for Me and you. These are the people I need you to exhort.'

"Moses called together the elders of the people and told them everything..." The only way Moses could tell them everything is because he trusts them. Whenever you're leading people in your life, a problem arises when you have people around you who are close to you but who you do not trust. In this transitional season, it is time to replace them. You do not have time to be wondering while the battle is going on if they are for you or against you. If you can spot Judas, hang him before he hangs you. This is not about your feelings right now. This is not about them getting hurt. It's about destiny. It is not personal, but at the same time, it is personal because you're trying to go somewhere. Therefore, it is also, business.

The reason some people cannot advance to where they need to go is because when they love people they want to give them a chance; but, when they see that things are not working out, they are unable to say, 'You know what? Thank you for coming, but right now I recognize that you cannot go where I am going because I don't trust you.' You have to know who is around you when you begin to share what the Lord said. Remember, if God wanted it to be public, He would have told everybody. Sometimes, when God speaks to us in private that conversation (word) is not for everybody.

If you get a word from the Lord, don't jump up saying, 'Ooh, I received a word from the Lord.' No, that was a word for you, not for the crowd. You have to know when God is speaking to you and who God wants you to share that message with. In this particular case, God said, 'I want everybody. Use the hierarchy you set up to get the word out. Go back, call a meeting, and talk to those around you whom you trust.' So Moses returns to a meeting, but second…

b) The leaders Relayed the Message. Verse 7 says, *"So Moses returned from the mountain and called together the elders of the people and told them everything the Lord had commanded him, and all the people responded together."* How do I know the leaders did their job? Because all the people responded. That's how I know that this process, this system, this protocol worked. Every single person responded. That means everybody Moses had on his dream team did their job and shared the message.

The people responded and said, *"We will do everything the Lord has commanded."* When you convey the Lord's message to the people you trust, make sure the communication is clear. Make it so clear that they can transfer the same information to the people who are responsible. If you are leading, if you are the Moses, you have to make sure that you can not only trust the people, but that you can get your ego out of the way and not feel like you are the only one who can relay or convey a message. Keep in mind, the reason God gave you the people is because the people have something they can offer you and there's something you can offer the people. If your ego gets in the way and you think you're the only one who can do everything, you're going to stunt everybody around you.

It is dangerous to have people in your life who you do not trust, because when that message comes and is conveyed out, not everyone is going to get the message the way you delivered it. Have you ever played the game "Telephone" where you're sitting at one end of the row and you whisper something to the person who is sitting next to you? The person next to you whispers the same thing to the person sitting next to him, and so on, until the message gets to the last person on the row. By the time it gets to the end of the row the whole message is different. Something happened between one person sharing and the other person receiving.

In this case, Moses and the elders were on one accord. Nobody was giving wrong information. You have to make sure that the people around you, in this season and in the next season in your life, receive clear communication, because communication is very important. Husbands, talk to your wives. Make sure everything is clear. Wives, talk to your husbands. Parents, talk to your children. Bosses, talk to your employees. Be clear in your communication. If things are not clear, at least make sure you are not at fault. Confusion happens when there is no clarity.

The people responded mutually to the clear communication from Moses and the elders. They said, 'We are going to do everything that the Lord says.'

Notice the words, *"...that the Lord says..."* Did the Lord talk to them? Yes, He did. The Lord imparted to His leader His Word. His leader imparted God's Word to his leaders. And through those leaders, the people heard the voice of God. When people don't follow protocol, they can miss God because they do not want to report only to the leader. When you skip protocol, you begin to get out of order. That happens because leaders sometimes have people they cannot trust in their organization or because people in leadership do not share the same heart as the leader. And when the followers are dealing with people like that, they don't know what God just said so they start doing their own thing.

But in this case, verse 8 says, *"And all the people responded together."*

3. He Was Encouraged With Validation

After he received the impartation and delivered the exhortation, Moses was encouraged with validation. God said, 'Moses, I have to confirm you in front of the people. I have to validate your leadership because I am doing something important.' Look at verse 9: *"After Moses climbed back up that mountain to talk to God and give the Lord the people's response, the Lord said to Moses, I will come to you in a thick cloud, Moses, so the people themselves can hear me when I speak with you, then they will always trust you."*

Here are three ways Moses was validated:

a) God showed a Sign. He came to Moses in a cloud. The people knew what that cloud signified. That cloud was the same signal that guided them through the Red Sea. That cloud represented the presence of God.

b) The people heard a Sound. Verse 9 says, *"...so the people themselves can hear me when I speak with you..."* Apparently, up until this point, the people had not heard God speaking to Moses. God had spoken to the people only through Moses. Now God says, 'I am about to take the mute off and I'm about to put everybody on a conference call so they will know that I have been talking to you in private. Now I want all of them to understand it was Me all along; and I am going to confirm that whatever comes out of your mouth has been coming out of My mouth. I am going to show everybody that you know Me. I want to be sure that they hear Me for themselves and do not miss what I have said and so end up adding their own thing to it.'

This display helps purge the people's motives as now there is no excuse for anybody not to understand that what Moses said is what God has been saying the whole time. God says, 'I know that they are a little slow, they are a little stubborn, because they won't listen to you, but now, they are going to hear everything that has been spoken in private directly from Me.'

c) The people showed their Support. Verse 9 says, *"...they will always trust you."* A sign of trust is support. If you trust somebody you will support them. Even if you support them a little that means you trust them a little. At least if you have some kind of support you have some level of trust and if you have some level of support that means that level of trust can grow. Right now, God is saying, Moses, I want to make sure that I validate you, so the people will now look at you and say, 'You know what? We want to know God like he knows God so we can get closer.'

The responsibility of those of us who know God and talk to God is that we have to be careful that we do not put ourselves in the place of God. You may not know everything about the Bible; you may not know all the Greek and Hebrew, but if somebody comes to you and wants to know how to read their Bible, or wants to learn how to pray, or wants to know and understand when God speaks, you have to be careful that you don't give them your interpretation of the Scripture, or your understanding of how to pray, or your experience of when God speaks. You should give them a Bible and tell them, Go, read it, and study it, and come back and tell me what you understand and then we'll discuss it.' You have to make sure they end up talking with God for themselves, and then you guide them through. If you're not careful, you will become their god and every time they are having trouble they're coming to you instead of going to God. If you're not careful, you can put yourself in the place of God and have people depending on you, and then you start walking around with the big head, and God will not be pleased.

God wants to bring about validation so the people who follow you will end up understanding God for themselves.

4. They All Experienced a Visitation

How did they experience a visitation?
a) There was **necessary preparation.**
b) There was a **season of consecration.**
c) There was a **spirit of expectation.**
d) There was a **glorious manifestation.**

Verse 10 says, *"Then the Lord told Moses, go down and prepare the people for my arrival."* What God is saying is, 'If you want to experience Me in a way you have never experienced Me before, you have to, first of all, ***get prepared*** for Me. You have to act like you are about to go somewhere special. You have to act like you want Me to come. I don't want you any kind of way when I find you. I need you to make sure that if you want Me to speak into your life like I have never spoken into your life before, you must prepare yourself.'

Not only is there a season of preparation, but there is also a:

a) Season of Consecration. Consecration means setting yourself apart. Looking at verse 10 again: *"...the Lord told Moses, go down and prepare the people for my arrival. Consecrate them today, and tomorrow, and have them wash their clothing."* Don't delay this. Consecration starts today. God says, 'Have them wash their clothes. I want them dressed appropriately when I show up. What they are wearing is symbolic of who they are; they are pure. They ought to take time to look good in My presence—not just externally, but internally. They ought to consecrate not just their clothes but who they are on the inside. Make sure you start your season of consecration today. You don't need to go on a forty-day fast for this, Moses. I need you to start it today.

There also needs to be a:

b) Spirit of Expectation. Look at verse 11: *"Be sure they are ready on the third day."* 'Be sure that they expect Me to show up like I say I am going to show up and do what I say I am going to do. Make sure they are ready for it and not trying to get ready.' God says, 'I am ready to show up in their lives. Make sure they are ready to receive Me when I come. If they are not consecrated, if they are dirty, if they have been distracted, then, when I show up, they are going to miss what I am trying to do in their lives. Right now, it is so important, I need you to make sure they have a spirit of expectation; that they are looking for Me these next few days.'

Finally, a:

c) Glorious Manifestation. Looking again at verse 11: *"Be sure they are ready on the third day for on that day, the Lord will come down."* He gave them the exact day He would come down. He's going to manifest Himself. The people had two days for consecration: today and tomorrow. On the third day, God would manifest like never before.

This occurs in the month of August, the eighth month of the year. The number eight is the number for new beginnings. Some things ended in July and new things are beginning in August. That is why God said, 'I need you to get ready,' because the season is about to change. He says, *"on the third day."* 'In fact, you don't have to wait for the third day because today I can manifest. I don't have to go through all that stuff because I am God. If you came ready today, I can manifest today. If you're not ready, I'm going to give you some time to get ready, and if you're ready by Tuesday, I'm ready to reveal Myself in your life like never before.'

Right now, you have to make sure that you let nothing in the next few days get in the way of you getting closer to God. That means there are some things you have to cut out, some things you have to stop, some things you have to get away from. Somebody might get mad but don't worry about it, you'll talk to them on Wednesday. If you're after something, you can let the television go, you can let the food go, you can let some stuff go in order to get closer to God.

God says, 'I want to speak to you because there are some things you've been asking for years and I want to give you the answers.' You don't have any money, but God wants to show you how to get the business. God wants to show you how to get your family back. That's what God is doing. Manifesting Himself. God's manifestation will bring answers, clarity, and direction.

The next few days of your life are very important. If you just read this book, you're going to miss God. If you really need God to speak in your life, if you've really need God to direct you, I already see Him giving this revelation to you. God does not really have to give you money; He can give you an idea. Pray right now for ideas, because right now you do not have any idea of how you are going to get out of your situation. Pray right now for God to manifest an idea in your mind. God will begin to open up doors for your business. God will open up doors for your family. God will open up doors for your ministry. God is about to speak to those who are ready to listen.

Pray right now: God, I receive Your revelation in advance.

> Exactly two months after the Israelites left Egypt, they arrived in the wilderness of Sinai. After breaking camp at Rephidim, they came to the wilderness of Sinai and set up camp there at the base of Mount Sinai.
>
> Then Moses climbed the mountain to appear before God. The Lord called to him from the mountain and said, "Give these instructions to the family of Jacob; announce it to the descendants of Israel: 'You have seen what I did to the Egyptians. You know how I carried you on eagles' wings and brought you to myself. Now if you will obey me and keep my covenant, you will be my own special treasure from among all the peoples on earth; for all the earth belongs to me. And you will be my kingdom of priests, my holy nation.' This is the message you must give to the people of Israel."
>
> So Moses returned from the mountain and called together the elders of the people and told them everything the Lord had commanded him. And all the people responded together, "We will do everything the Lord has commanded." So Moses brought the

people's answer back to the Lord.

Then the Lord said to Moses, "I will come to you in a thick cloud, Moses, so the people themselves can hear me when I speak with you. Then they will always trust you."

Moses told the Lord what the people had said. Then the Lord told Moses, "Go down and prepare the people for my arrival. Consecrate them today and tomorrow, and have them wash their clothing. Be sure they are ready on the third day, for on that day the Lord will come down on Mount Sinai as all the people watch."

Exodus 19:3-11 (NLT)

Focus Verse: Verse 3: "Then Moses climbed the mountain to appear before the Lord."